Jack And Me:
How *Not* To Live After Loss

JACK AND ME:
HOW *NOT* TO LIVE
AFTER LOSS
COSMO LANDESMAN

THE **BLACK SPRING**
PRESS GROUP

First published in 2022

Eyewear Publishing, an imprint of The Black Spring Press Group

Grantully Road, Maida Vale, London W9

United Kingdom

Cover art Andrew Magee

Typesetting User Design, Illustration and Typesetting, UK

Printing Short Run Press, Devon, UK

ISBN-13 978-1-915406-16-3

To Jack, with love.

Dad x

Contents

1

Jack Comes Home

London, July 2015

Today I went to my local funeral parlour to collect my son Jack's ashes and bring them home. The funeral director handed me a beige cloth bag and inside was the plastic urn containing Jack's ashes. It felt odd carrying that bag along the Islington High Street in the sunshine on a Saturday morning – as if I were just another dad carrying the shopping home. I was in fact a dad carrying the remains of his son who, a few weeks earlier, had committed suicide.

In theory it was a solemn moment, one demanding serious reflection on the tragedy of my son's death. But the comic potential of the situation kept coming to mind. (After all, a classic comic sketch in films and T.V. sit-coms is when the urn of death is subjected to the slapstick of life.) What if I took a tumble and out spilled Jack, his urn rolling down the pavement and into the road and rolling-on ahead? (*Cabbie! Follow that urn!*) Or what if I left him on the bus? I gripped the bag tighter and walked slower.

Once at home I said to Jack's urn: "where the hell do I put you?"

The obvious place was on the mantelpiece, in the front room. But I feared it would dominate the room and make it look too shrine like. Guests would wonder what that curious plastic thing was, and then feel embarrassed when I told them.

So where do I put Jack's ashes? I consider the options, and they're all bad.

I could put them in my bedroom – no, too spooky.

I could put them in the kitchen – no, too casual.

I could put them in the loo (like they were death's Oscar?) – no, too kitschy.

Unable to make a decision I tuck the urn bag under the coat stand in the hall and that's where I leave him. Finding a place for Jack's ashes became another domestic task on my To Do List that never gets done.

● ● ●

My problem with Jack's ashes wasn't really about where to put them; I just couldn't face taking the urn out of the bag and having to touch it, look at it or talk to it. And then I realised I'd – once again – turned my back on Jack, shoved him out of sight and out of mind when his presence proved too difficult to deal with.

Then one day I decided to just do it. I go and grab the bag, take it to the kitchen, pull it out and place the urn on the kitchen table. On its plastic screw-top is a white sticker that reads: Cremated Remains of the Late Jack Landesman, 17 July 2015. My first impulse is to leave it at that, but I want to peek inside and see Jack so I start to unscrew the lid…and then I stop.

No. I'm not ready for you. Not yet. Sorry Jack.

I decide to put the urn on the shelf in the right hand corner of the sitting room where he can be seen, but is not on prominent display. (Jack never liked being the centre of attention.) So I clear a little space for him amongst the books and tuck him up in that cosy corner. I can see him. I can talk to him. I can give him a little dust from time to time.

"Welcome home Jack," I say.

• • •

But at some point Jack's ashes got moved from his cosy corner to inside the small cupboard space beneath the bookshelves – the one crammed with forgotten DVDs, old rock magazines, audio-cassettes, defunct phone chargers, a broken guitar tuner and all the other detritus of a past Jack and I once shared. I think I first put him out of sight because I had a succession of Airbnb guests staying and when they were gone…I don't know…I never took him out again. It was easier – emotionally – having him stashed away out of sight. And there he has remained these past seven years; the skeleton in my cupboard.

I haven't kept Jack as close to me as I thought I would. In my funeral eulogy in 2015 I said that in life I had lost him, but now I felt that I had found him again and I would never let him go. But I did. I have rejected the rituals of remembrance: I don't do anything special on Jack's birthday or the anniversary of his death.

Of course I haven't forgotten him totally, I just don't spend much time remembering him. I thought that was a good sign. It showed that I'd made my peace with Jack; but I'd only pushed him away. It wasn't closure; it was an act of cowardice. I couldn't face Jack because I couldn't face my guilt and all my regrets. And I couldn't face the simple fact he was gone forever.

Like the idea of infinity, forever is impossible to grasp, especially when forever involves the loss of someone you have loved. It's just too big; this absence without end. So, when I think about Jack being gone forever this is what I think: I will never, ever walk into my living room again and see Jack look up from his laptop and give me that little Jack head-nod of recognition and hear him softly say, "hey, how's it going?".

• • •

But now, coming back to this book has brought him back into my head. His voice, his music, his smell, his mad infuriating Jackness is back and with it, all the grief and guilt it provokes in me. I don't want that anymore. I don't want to hide him in a cupboard and keep him out of mind. I want to be able to remember Jack, talk about Jack, talk to Jack and see photos of Jack and not feel that sudden drizzle of sadness or that energy sapping guilt I usually get. I want Jack out of the cupboard and back in my life.

So, I'm going to have to go and retrieve the urn from its hiding place – and rescue Jack from being pushed further and further into the past by the passage of time. All I have to do is go upstairs, enter my sitting room, open the cupboard, grab the urn and bring Jack down to be with me in my study. But I won't be able to do that unless I write this book – or I should say, rewrite this book. I won't be able to find a place for Jack in my life unless I find a life after loss.

Then And Now

When I began the first version of this book in the months that followed Jack's death in June 2015, I was adamant: no life lessons. No advice. No comforting truths. I had no wisdom to offer, but plenty of guilt, grief, hurt, shame, self-disgust and anger to share with readers.

Here's what I wrote back then:

"Does the world really need another 'moving' memoir of the death of a father, mother, spouse, sibling or child by cancer, accident or suicide? The kind of memoir where the author is praised for their "bravery" and "honesty" in facing that thing we fear the most: the loss of a loved one. This book is not one of those books – the kind that offers feel-good-grief with their mawkish mix of misery and happy memories all wrapped-up and resolved in a nice pink bow of comforting closure. Fuck that. This is not one for all you grief vampires who feed on the tragedies of others."

I went on:

"I guess you could say that his death was tragic – but like all suicides it was selfish, cruel and worse of all: unnecessary. So please don't be moved by my son's suicide. Get your own dead kid to grieve over. Shake your head in disbelief at the sheer stupidity of what he did – and be disgusted at what I didn't do to save him. Don't feel sorry for Jack and don't feel sorry for me. I don't want your fucking sympathy. The truth is: I don't deserve your sympathy".

That was the angry voice of my grief talking; a nasty, unfeeling, stupid and self-incriminating voice that now causes me to wince when I hear it. But at the time I thought I was telling the truth. My book was going to be more honest than all the other books about loss. Unlike the grief sentimentalists who told it like it wasn't, I was the no-bullshit-truth-teller who had the courage to face the Big Nothing of loss.

I had what I thought was a terrible but necessary message for those grieving and it was this: the death of your child, your wife, your husband, the one you love is nothing more than a cruel and arbitrary event, one devoid of meaning and mercy.

Most articles and memoirs on loss that I read offered the Truth of Hope; that something positive and life-affirming can come out of a terrible event. From America came the idea of post-traumatic *growth*, which is the belief that grief can enrich our lives emotionally, spiritually and socially. Death had been co-opted into the personal growth movement. Loss, I was now being told, was a learning experience.

Against the Truth of Hope, I offered the Truth of Despair: you can't change anything, learn anything or do anything – so just grit your teeth and suffer in silence. I called my approach Silent Stoicism and was in direct opposition to the prevailing practice of Suicide Activism.

After Jack died I would read about other parents who, following the suicide of their child, became suicide activists; crusaders who had a cause that gave their shattered life a new meaning and purpose. They devoted themselves to raising public awareness about suicide and mental health issues. They set up suicide prevention charities while others ran marathons and baked biscuits to raise money for established charities like CALM and the Maytree Respite Centre.

I believed there was no comfort or meaning to be gained from such activities. But then, I didn't want comfort or meaning; I wanted pain and misery. I wanted my grief to be raw and visceral, undiluted by good works. My pain would, I believed, keep me connected to my son. I tried to explain to people that we must take care of our grief and not try to tame it, domesticate it or let it teach us fuzzy feel-good truths. When people mentioned the word "closure" I would snort derisively and say: "fuck closure". I want my wound raw and open. Hurt is my hotline to my dead boy.

And now here I am seven years later and I'm thinking; what if I got it all wrong? Did I miss a great opportunity to make something good out of Jack's death – for me and for other people in my place? Had I not been so angry and cynical maybe I could have written or said a few words that might have made a difference to some suicidal kid like mine or some grieving parent like me. Instead, I spent seven years sitting on my arse doing nothing but writing a book about how there is no life after loss. I'm hoping that this book will prove me wrong.

2

That Moment

It's said that the death of a child is every parent's worst nightmare. It is, but there's one big and obvious difference between nightmares and the loss of a child: you wake-up from nightmares. Your dead child is dead forever.

I remember that before Jack died I would read in newspapers about some teenager who killed himself and think, "How terrible! Their poor parents! What must that be like?" And then one day it was my turn to be one of the poor parents we read about. And tomorrow, it will be someone else's turn. As I write this – and as you read it – somebody's child is probably in their bedroom making preparations to kill themselves.

People said to me after Jack died, "I can't imagine what that must be like" – by which they mean that precise moment you first get the news that your child is dead. Actually, they can – but they just don't want to. Who can blame them? It's too terrible a thought to entertain. But they are curious. We all are. It's like watching a horror film of your worst nightmare happen to someone else, from the safety of your life.

So, what's it like that moment you get the news that your child is dead?

It's like one of those big moments of history that shakes the world, but it's your history and your little world that gets shaken.

People of my generation say they remember exactly where they were when President Kennedy was shot – or people remember the exact moment when they first saw the planes go into the twin towers on 9/11. Well, it's a bit like that, only you're the one that gets shot; you're the building that comes under attack.

At first it's something too big and too terrible to fully take in; you are inoculated from immediate and total devastation by your incomprehension. But wait. It's only a matter of time before your inner world – which for the moment is wobbly but intact – comes crashing down and you're left alone wandering around in the rubble of your new life.

• • •

I got the news of Jack's death on the 29th of June 2015 while I was on a holiday cruise ship somewhere in the Mediterranean. (I was writing a travel feature for the *Sunday Times*, where I wrote a dating column for *Style* magazine.) I'd made plans for three days of hedonistic abandonment when on day one I get a Facebook message from Poria Cyrus, an old friend of Jack's, wanting my phone number so that, "we can speak as soon as possible."

Instantly I know this must be about Jack and I message back: "Does Jack need help?"

Poria replies that he wants to speak about Jack and asks when I'm back in the UK? He's clearly worried about Jack. I figure that they'd probably met up and Jack had talked about wanting to kill himself and Poria is freaked out and thinks he'd better tell Jack's parents what's going on. He probably doesn't know that his parents know all about Jack's suicide attempts. But we do. I know them so well I don't worry about them anymore – at least not the way I used to or perhaps should.

• • •

I know what you're thinking: what kind of parent doesn't worry about their child's suicide threats? How does that happen? Answer: Life happens. At first the word suicide itself is so shocking and scary, but over time it loses its power to scare. It gets assimilated into the fabric of daily life and becomes a familiar feature of your child's story. One minute you're talking with your kid about suicide and later that evening you're talking about ordering a takeaway. And like the boy in the fable who cried wolf too many times, Jack threatened suicide too many times. He talked about it too much. Made jokes about it too much. And so did I. We did suicide banter together.

So I wasn't worried even though I knew that Jack had tried suicide a few times. But the gravity of those attempts were undermined by the passage of time and the farcical failure of his efforts. Jack takes a heroin overdose, and gets a mere nose bleed. Jack tries to hang himself – but the hook on the back of the door breaks. Jack plans to jump from a tall building – but can't find the exit door to the ledge. (None of these attempts resulted in any kind of physical injury or need for medical attention.) There was a kind of *Harold and Maude* black comedy to Jack's suicide attempts. I use to joke: thank God Jack is too incompetent to kill himself!

Yeah, it's not so funny now.

Reading over Poria's message I think: screw Jack! He's not going to mess up my holiday! I badly need this break from my London life and I need a break from Jack and all his problems and all my worries about his problems and the biggest problem of them all: Jack and me.

My Jack, Your Jack

What was my Jack like? Lots of parents have a Jack in their life. He can be any age or any sex. But the Jacks of this world are lost, lonely, depressed, often on drugs and off the grid of adulthood. They are full of hurt and anger and self-hatred. They are impossible to live with and impossible to let go of. And their poor loving parents don't know what the hell to do about them.

You might have seen my Jack around. He's that tall young man peering out from his black hoodie – the one with the torn jeans, the split trainers, and the stained Slipknot T-shirt. His face is unshaven, unclean; his skin is blotchy and seeing his long dirty dreads – yes, another white boy with dreads! – sends a shiver of yuckiness down your spine. There are crumbs of sleep gunk in the corner of his tired eyes. Sometimes he carries a black dustbin bag full of all his worldly goods as he wanders across the streets of London looking for shelter.

He's that guy who approaches you on the street and asks you for spare change to get a bus/some food/a place in a hostel for the night. At times he could look scary; at times he could look sweet. You might have seen him on a park bench trying to sleep or curled up on the pavement with his head bowed. Weeping. Another Lost Boy with no way back home.

And you shake your head and think: *that's somebody's son*!
Yeah, it is! That trampy looking creature who begs for money? That
was my son. That was my Jack. Or I should say: that's the Other
Jack. The Jack he became in his late teens; the one I couldn't
stand. Parents don't always have to like their children, but they're
expected to always love them. Sometimes loving a Jack is hard –
and sometimes it's impossible.

Lone-Leee Jack

In my mind I see Jack and he's always alone; pacing back and forth
in the open cage of his solitude.

We don't teach our young how to deal with loneliness, because
we don't know how to deal with it ourselves. And we're embarrassed to admit that we're lonely too. That's the taboo nobody wants
to talk about or confess to. Loneliness belongs to losers, the social
failures – or at least that's what the lonely think. Nobody hates the
lonely like the lonely do; like Jack did. Loneliness was the bully
that always picked on him, even as a kid at school. But loneliness
doesn't want your lunch money; it wants your life. Jack once told
me that his greatest fear was that his parents would suddenly die
and he'd be left all alone.

Towards the end of his life when he was living in a small room
in Harrow, I knew Jack was lonely so I would invite him to come
to my flat for dinner or just come and hang out. He did and he was
still alone whether he was in my kitchen making tea or in my living
room, plugged into his battered laptop watching a film from the 70s
– usually something crazy starring Dennis Hopper – or listening to

one of his beloved nu-metal bands – Bile, Korn or Slipknot. I could hear their tinny insect rage seeping out from his headphones.

Sometimes I'd be sitting on my own when from a distant room I'd hear the cry of, *"Lone-leee! Lone-leee!"*

It's Jack. He did this from time to time. He sits on his own and suddenly cries out, *"Lone-leeee"* and he does it in the voice of Kermit the Frog. It's comic and tragic at the same time. And then he goes silent. An hour or maybe two hours later I will hear it again: *"Lone-leeeee!"*

And then silence.

And then there was Jack's smell. It was the smell that assaulted me in the morning when I walked into the living room whenever he slept over on my sofa bed. It wasn't the usual teenage boy smell that comes from a fetid cocktail of trainers and socks and sweaty t-shirts. Jack wasn't a teenager; but a young adult and too old for that kind of smell. (And he kept himself clean.) No, Jack's smell was of a life that had gone off. (A friend who had let Jack stay with her said she knew that smell of his and thought it was a detoxing-from-drugs kind of smell.) To me it had the slight whiff of putrefaction.

I can remember Jack's baby smell: that warm, milky powdery scent of new-born skull and skin; the Chanel No.5 of creation.

Jack hated it when I referred to his Jack smell or made jokes about it. For a boy completely indifferent to his appearance he was very touchy about his smell. I could tell that he was hurt by my cries of, *"Phew!"* and *"Pongo-City!"*

He'd say: Man, do you have to be so cruel?

And sometimes I'd say: Do you have to stink-up the place?

And sometimes I just said: Sorry, Jack.

And now I wish I'd said nothing about his smell, especially in the light of what happened. On the 25th of June 2015 in a house in Harrow, it was the smell of Jack that led his housemates to discover his decomposing body, slumped on his bedroom floor.

3

Life After Loss

I'm possibly the last person in the world who should be writing a book about seeing life after loss in a positive way. I was angry, nihilistic, pessimistic, cynical and melancholic – even before Jack's death. (As a child my mother called me Eeyore.) To be honest, I'm not sure I have any wisdom or insights to offer anyone. When I first wrote this book I made a solemn vow: no life lessons! No uplifting truths or sound advice for suffering souls!

But here's what I've discovered: there are things worse than feeling awkward, appearing soft and sentimental and there are things even worse than offering life lessons. And the main one is doing nothing. Whether we fail or succeed in helping those with suicidal thoughts or people dealing with loss is not the point; at the end of the day we have to *try* and make a difference. Try and fail is always better than fail to try.

So Here's My Life Lesson Number One: *Be Kind*

There I said it. I can't believe I could write something so banal and trite; but I believe it! Aldous Huxley once wrote that he was embarrassed that after a lifetime of trying to understand the human condition the only advice this very clever man could offer was, "try to be a little kinder."

I know that kindness has become a panacea for all the problems of the world; the simple solution offered by simple minds. But I'm only making small claims for small acts of kindness. Sometimes it's just dumb trying to be so clever that you fear stating the obvious. The greatest truths of life *are* obvious and clichéd – the trick is to see beyond the shell of obviousness to the inner core of wisdom.

Yes, the idea of being kind *is* simplistic to the point of being stupid – but it's the actual daily, living practice of being kind, that is the complex and challenging bit. It requires dedication, discipline and daily training like an athlete might do. You have to exercise your kindness muscle or your empathy goes all soft and flabby.

Of course, it's easy to say be kind – but how do you maintain kindness with kids like Jack who drive you crazy? You don't. You try and be as kind as you can be, one day at a time and one infuriating incident at a time. But you have to accept the fact there will be days when you think: fuck kindness! I'm fed up with this useless lump of a child! You will just have to accept there are days when you are a Monster Dad or a Monster Mum dealing with a Monster Child, and you long to kick them out of the house and kick them out of your heart! It's ok. Don't feel guilty. Just don't do it. Be kind instead. Believe me, in the event of a tragedy you'll save yourself a lot of regret later on.

4

Lost At Sea

2015

The next morning, I find another Facebook message from Poria, asking for the phone number of Jack's mother and when will I be back in the UK.

I haven't spoken to Jack for nearly a week. He's not returned my texts or phone messages, which is unusual but not a cause for alarm. I figure he's lost his phone or has no credit or is pissed-off with me and/or the world. It's just a normal Jack thing.

I didn't tell Jack I was going on holiday because I didn't want him to ask if he could stay in my flat while I was away. I didn't want to come home to a messy flat and find Jack wrapped up in his dingy duvet, on the sofa watching YouTube videos (just as he had been doing five days ago before I left!) and then get into a fight about why the flat is in such a mess – as we had done before – and he would say, "What mess?" and I would point to the cups of half drunk tea, his clothes on the floor, the little pile of tobacco next to the torn rizla packet – clearly he's been smoking dope which I said he mustn't do in my flat – and he would say, "Dad, chill. You're being neurotic" and that would really piss me off even more than returning to a messy flat.

A kinder me would have said: Hey Jack, I'm away for a bit do you want to stay in my flat? That simple act of kindness could have saved his life. Jack had friends in my neighbourhood he could have hung-out with, but none where he lived in Harrow. And if he had no credit on his Oyster card, which was often the case, he couldn't travel anywhere to see anyone. So while I was on my luxury cruise Jack was probably trapped in his little white cube of a room. Of course, I can't be certain that letting Jack stay at my place would have saved his life – but neither can I rule it out.

• • •

I message Poria asking if he knows why Jack hasn't been in contact with me? And Poria messages back: "I'd rather speak on the phone."

Could this be it? That terrible thing I've been both dreading and denying would ever happen for the past five years? I know I'm *really* worried because I keep telling myself: *don't worry*! I reassure myself with reasons why there's nothing to worry about. The last time we spoke – eight days ago – Jack was trying to get a job cleaning windows, and was even asking my friends for references. That isn't the action of someone planning suicide. No, this is just another Jack scare. I'll call Poria and straighten this thing out and then get back to having fun.

And then Tessa – an old girlfriend who had been looking after Jack – is now trying to contact me on Facebook. Now *that's* scary. Unable to make contact with her or Poria from the phone in my cabin, I go to the reception desk to see if they can make the call for me. I explain to one of the staff that I need him to make an emergency phone call to London for me and he does. "It's ringing," he says and hands me the phone.

The First Time

The first time Jack ever mentioned suicide was one afternoon in 2010. He was in my flat and we were having tea and discussing Jack's favourite topics: My Shit Life. My Loneliness. My Suffering. My Fucked This and my Unbearable That. And then out it popped: *Yesterday, I tried to kill myself.*

Jack didn't say it in a melodramatic way; it sounded like just another bit of an ordinary day in the life of Jack. No more significant than, today I went shopping/saw a mate/got the bus/signed-on/ got stoned…

And oh yeah, I tried to kill myself.

No biggie.

This was the first time the word suicide came into Jack's story. It hit me like a surprise slap in the face from a passing stranger. I knew Jack had, since his teens, suffered from depression and anxiety. His use and abuse of drugs had landed him in an expensive rehab centre after hearing voices telling him he was going to hell. He'd dropped out of university after a series of panic attacks and then dropped out of life. So, I knew my son was a bit screwed-up; but I had no idea that he was this screwed-up. I mean, suicide screwed-up. It doesn't get more serious and screwed-up than that.

Till that moment I'd assumed that with the right medication, large doses of therapy, parental support and love – and Jack getting off his lazy arse and making some changes to his life – he'd be OK. His condition was not something life-threatening; he wasn't like one of those suicide kids. No. Jack was going through a difficult phase in his life. People do. But he was going to be alright. Nothing bad would happen to Jack because his mum and I would look after him, watch his back and get him through this bad patch.

But Jack's talk of suicide changes everything. A line has been crossed and his little lump of misery is now malignant: life threatening. Suddenly, I am a dad with a suicidal son. How the hell did that happen? And more importantly: what the hell do I do now? Call a doctor? An ambulance? His mum?

No, says Jack. Don't tell mum. (She lives in Brighton with her husband.) He doesn't want her to worry and says she's got enough on her plate, what with her husband not being well.

And I think: Oh, as long as we don't upset mummy we can just freak out daddy with impunity. Thanks Jack!

I see now that you weren't being insensitive but kind and protective. You were more concerned with your mum's feelings and welfare than your own. You didn't want to be a burden of worry to her. I get it. You were a good boy.

Jack, did I ever tell you that? I probably did and you probably got embarrassed and muttered: *yeah, cheers*.

And how did I react to Jack's suicide announcement? I take a deep breath and tell myself to stay calm. He needs a calm dad that can help him. A figure he can trust and turn to. So I slip into what I call my Doctor Cosmo mode. I take on the calm demeanour of the mental health professional.

Ok Jack, I say, let's talk about this. And Jack, stretched out on the sofa tells me, "I think about suicide all the time now", and I sit in my armchair and stroke my chin in a pose of deep thoughtfulness. I ask questions and probe my patient gently, always responding with encouraging nods and I say, "I see" and "I understand." In short, I do everything I can to hide the fact from my poor suicidal son that I'm so scared and I haven't the faintest idea what the hell to do now.

What's A Dad To Do?

In retrospect, I know what I should have done. Every dad knows what to do when your son says he wants to die: you put your hands on his shoulder, you look him straight in the eye and then you give them the big speech. The one about how, "I love you – you know that!" and how, "Together we're going to beat this thing." And you wrap your arms around him in a big hug and he wraps his arms around you and he starts to cry. And in your arms this weeping mess of a young man is your little boy again who needs his big, strong dad. He breaks down and weeps and you tighten the hug, like it was a tourniquet to stop the emotional bleeding. And you say, "It's going to be Ok…you're going to be Ok. I promise."

Now it's your turn to cry. And you don't want to cry. Dad's don't cry. (That's crap and you know it!) But anyway, you try to hold back the tears but they burst through and out they pour. And this provokes another round of tears from him – which really sets you off now. All restraint, all that talk of being the strong dad is dissolved by the hot lava of your tears. You are a big, quivering, blubbering, shaking mess of a man.

"Now look at what you've done, you bastard!" you say and you both start laughing.

And then feeling a little self-conscious you let go of each other with a final pat on the back and then you will say to your weeping suicidal son, "Fancy a cup of tea?" and he smiles and says, "Yeah, go on."

But I didn't do it then. (What I did do was book an appointment for us to go see his doctor.) I never just gave him a big hug and said, I love you and I will always be there for you. (Or maybe I did and I don't remember?) If I didn't, why didn't I? Was it embarrassment or that awkwardness that we always had around each other? Or was it something worse: the absence of love?

Here's Life Lesson Number Two: *Hug Them*

Just hug them. Just keep hugging them and let them know how much you love them. Do it every day. Three times a day: morning, noon and night. Make them beg for you to stop hugging them; to stop telling them you love them. Watch them run out of the living room screaming, "Not the hug I-love-you-thing! Please Dad, stop! I beg you!"

Put this book down now and go do it. Go straight to that child with all the problems and dark thoughts, the one you worry about late at night in bed and stops you from sleeping – go right now and hold and hug them and declare your love. Cover them in kisses and tell them you will never let them go! And when they squirm and try to break free, hold them tighter and hug them harder.

Reader, I have a question: does this sound stupid? Am I talking complete crap? Have I gone from knee-jerk cynicism to icky senti-mentalism? I once hated all this sort of mawkish stuff and now look at me! Anyway, let's ask Jack what he thinks of my life lessons.

Jack: Dude, where do you get this huggy-wuggy shit from? What's going on inside that head of yours? Dad, are you on drugs? This is some silly-crazy shit! I really don't know what to say – you need help. Honest. You can't write this sort of stuff; people will think you're more fucked-up than I was!

Me: Ok Jack. What do you advise parents to do with…you know, kids like you?

Jack: Oh that's easy. They don't need your fucking hugs; they need your help to die! That's all you have to do. It's really simple. Show them that you truly love them and help them to end the fucking pain and suffering of their miserable shit existence!

Me: Boy, that brings back memories! You said that to me a hundred times. And what did I say to you?

Jack: Oh you know, life can be so good…la-la-la…you can change…blah, blah, blah…try and be positive…suicide is not the answer…and all that other shit.

Me: I said I can help you to live, but I will never help you to die.

Jack: Whatever.

Me: By the way, nobody says whatever anymore.

Jack: Really? Ok. Whatever!

• • •

Meanwhile Back at Sea: Just Three Words.

Everything in your life can change in three seconds with just three words. That's what happened to me when the ship's receptionist handed me the phone.

Tessa says, "Hello Cos".

One…

Me: Hey Tessa, what's up?

Tessa: Oh Cos, Jack is gone!

Two…

I don't know what she means by gone. Gone missing?

Me: What do you mean?

Three…

Tessa: Jack is dead.

And there it is. Three words. Jack. Is. Dead.

Boom.

• • •

I want to talk to people and explain to them what has happened. I need a hug. I need someone to hold me and say they understand me and are going to help me. I need the kindness of strangers. But this is what I tell myself: *a holiday cruise ship is no place for a*

weeping dad. Nobody wants to hear your sad story about your sui-
cidal son. These people are on holiday, they don't want some true-
life horror story from a stranger. So do everyone a favour and take
your tears and your trauma and go back to your cabin: quarantine
your sorrow.

So I'm in my shoebox of a cabin. It's cute, colourful, com-
pact; like a cell in a progressive open prison. It offers sanctuary
from everything except me and my mind. I feel dazed. Wobbly.
Confused. Like I've had a head injury. I've been mugged by life.

Jack did it! He actually did it! I can't believe it. I have to
believe it. Funny. You can't believe that they will ever do it – and
when they do it, you can't believe they've done it. Zed is dead.
Mr. Kurtz, he dead. And now Jack is dead. Fuck me! I have a dead
son! Nobody I know has a dead son. Their sons are at university or
starting their first real job or making plans to get married. But not
my son, not my Jack. He decided to do something different with his
life: end it.

• • •

I stretch out on the bed and wonder: what do I do now? I can't call
anyone in London from my cabin and I don't want to go back to
reception. I can't Google for answers and being an atheist I can't
turn to God for guidance or comfort. Now what? What's the proce-
dure for a suicide? What do you do? Sit and wait? (For what?) Read?
(Can't concentrate). Go for coffee? (Caffeine will make me even
more stressed.) Shower? (Why?) Take a nap? (Impossible.) Have a
wank? (Don't be so stupid!) I lay back on the bed and let it all wash
over me; my head is full of distress signals. Red flares that no one

can see are going off; cries of *Mayday! Mayday!* that no one but me can hear.

I am all alone.

Lost at sea.

5

Love & Grief

In Naples I abandoned ship to catch a flight from Naples Airport back home to London. At Stansted airport I'm greeted by my girl-friend Alice. She gives me a hug, wrapping her arms around me tightly like a bandage. Alice drives me to my flat in North London and I tell her what will become the familiar tale of my holiday on a pleasure cruise; the one with the surprise ending. During a silence Alice says, "You don't have to talk if you don't want to."

This is my first conversation as the new me – or I should say – the new perception of me. I sense that I'm no longer the old me that people once knew: Cosmo. Journalist. Dad. Nice guy. I'm now the man with the suicide son. I wonder what that will mean? At social occasions will people wonder if they should mention *it* – and will I wonder if I should mention *it*? How strange: I now have an It in my life. My very own big, potentially awkward and best-not-mention It.

In the car I spot an IKEA. "Let's stop here and pick up a coffin for Jack," I say. "On second thoughts, maybe not. I don't think we could figure out how to assemble it."

We exchange looks that say: too soon?

Alice offers to stay with me, but I know she has her kids to collect from school and things to do, so I insist she goes off. I'll be fine, I say, playing at being brave.

Now I'm alone. And being back home in my flat in Islington is comforting and disconcerting; it's as if I don't quite fit-in here. Everything looks familiar and yet feels kind of strange. I call it *death-lag:* it's that fuzzy-wobbly feeling you get when you travel between the time zones of before loss and after loss. I busy myself with small tasks of making tea, having a tidy-up, unpacking and waiting for my return to normality.

The first thing I want to do is call my close friends and tell them the news about Jack. I sit at my desk with my mobile phone and look at my Favourites List – and there at the top is Jack's name and number. I'm curious to find out what will happen if I call it. Will a voice say this number is no longer in service or invite me to leave a message? Maybe I will get some sort of spooky *Twilight Zone* encounter where a faint, crackly Jack-like voice says, "Hi dad". I can't use his number and I can't delete it.

● ● ●

It's such a relief to be off that floating fun fair and away from all those happy faces and families having fun. Now that I'm back home I can start to grieve properly. I can let go, take off my mask of normality, put away my smile and un-gag my heart and let the tears and hurt gush out. I can weep in the morning and weep late into the night. I can binge on guilt and regret. And I will rant at life, howl at the moon and rip out my broken bleeding heart and beg Jack for forgiveness. And I will keep crying and crying until there's nothing left; not one little salty tear.

But instead, I go to a private members' club in Soho and get pissed and take coke with an old friend.

• • •

When I arrived my friend greeted me with, "You look like a man who could use a blow-job!" (She wasn't offering, she was observing.) I know how that must sound to some readers: inappropriate, insensitive and inexcusable. But to me it was a brave and funny thing to say to a man who has just lost his son. It's what I wanted – no, not the blow-job – but just to be normal again. To be me before that me and my life got blown away on that ship. That's the thing about the suicide of a loved one: they die and they take you with them; you're collateral damage.

On returning home I wish I'd never gone out. I've got coke regret – "what a terrible fucking drug!" – and a head full of booze and a gut full of guilt. But where's my grief? I feel what I can only describe as emotional constipation. So I use music as a kind of emotional laxative, to loosen me up as it were.

Here Is My Spotify Grief Playlist

1   'Cat's in the Cradle' by Harry Chapin. This is the national anthem of all dads who torment themselves with their inadequacy. The song is about a super busy businessman dad who never had time for his son when the boy was growing-up. And then his son grows up and becomes a super busy adult and has no time for his dad. It's an anthem of parental regret; a beautiful hymn to father failure.

2   'Always On My Mind' by Elvis Presley. Elvis sings the lines, "maybe I didn't love you as often as I could have/maybe I didn't

treat you as good as I should have" with such a soft, under-stated sorrow that it's heart-breaking. When I hear the line, "But you were always on my mind" I change it in my head to, "But you were always on my tits!" Jack would have laughed. "Good one dad," – that's what he always said.

3   'Nature Boy' by Nat King Cole. There are dozens of versions of this classic. David Bowie did it and Massive Attack covered it in Baz Lurman's *Moulin Rouge*, but nothing compares with the Nat King Cole version. He sings the lines as if he's telling you a bedtime story: "there was a boy, a special boy/a little shy and sad of eye." The boy in the song tell us that, "the greatest thing you will ever learn is to love and be loved in return", which just about sums up exactly what I didn't do with Jack.

4   'Fire and Rain' by James Taylor. Ok, obvious choice but if hearing him sing "I've seen fire and I've seen rain…but I always thought I would see you again" doesn't get you blubbing, then you're dead too.

As I listen to the songs I go through old family photo albums and pull out pictures of Jack as a smiling baby and a happy little boy. I love the one with Jack sitting at the wheel of his big, red plastic car with the yellow top. (Better known as The Little Tikes Cosy Coupe.) He loved that car! And I have a photo of Jack in his bedroom. The one with the Disney's *Aladdin* wallpaper, the large *Jurassic Park* poster, the *Ninja Turtle's* dustbin and he's under his *Sonic the Hedgehog* duvet and he's smiling a smile so big it swallows up his face. Here is proof that I once had a happy boy – and that's some-thing I need to remember.

But the happy boy who made funny faces and struck silly poses before the camera is superseded by the awkward adolescent paralysed by self-consciousness. The photographs show Jack in his various pop culture incarnations. There's the cropped bleached white hair, the nose ring/lip ring and blank stare of his Eminem phase. This is followed a few years later by his Robert Smith of The Cure look. (That is mascara that were once his eyes.) To think that the smiling boy with the Krusty the Clown T-shirt has become the sullen teenager with the Insane Clown Posse t-shirt. And finally there's the photo of one Christmas with Jack and my new son and wife. We're opening presents. Everyone looks happy but Jack. He sits slumped on the sofa, a gun-like finger is pointed to the side of his head as he mimes blowing his brains out.

But the music and photos don't work their magic. I cry. A trickle of tears, not a torrent. Crying isn't good enough; it's too easy, too much a part of everyday life. Tears can be trite. I cry at schmaltzy films and dumb pop records. My son's death demands something bigger, something commensurate to the enormity of the event.

Sorry For Your Loss

But I'm soon distracted from my grief quest by the messages of condolence that start to pour in. My dating column for the *Sunday Times Style* magazine is a fun and frothy read about my disastrous attempts to find love. Readers like it. Now this. I'm not sure if you can write a frothy dating column with a dead child in the shadows.

Being a freelance journalist means I spend a lot of time –
at least in the day – on my own in front of a computer screen, trying
to write a piece or work on a project. Like every freelancer, a lot of
my time is spent checking for phone messages, emails and texts.
On a good day I will get one really good email; on a great day I get
two really good emails.

People not in the media imagine that media people enjoy this
glamorous metropolitan life of lunches and launches; it's all just
an endless swirl of exciting social events. You get the occasional
taste of that, but if you work from home like most freelance jour-
nalists and you're not super successful or famous, you just sit all
day in front of a computer screen thinking: *this is shit!…My piece is
shit!…Journalism is shit!…My life is shit! No one returns my calls…
no one texts me…I just sit here writing this shit piece and checking
my phone for calls and messages that never come.*

But now look! I've never had so many emails and texts. There's
at least a dozen messages of condolence. Dexter, my ten-year-old
son from my second marriage, writes: "Dear Dad, Mum has told
me the sad news about Jack" and that he loves me. Friends tell me
that they "love me" and are "there for me" and happy to "do anything for me". They want me "to call anytime", "come and have
lunch", "come and visit", take me "to a movie", "go for a walk",
"or we can just do nothing at all". My friend Jonathan Putzman
even offers to pay for me to go on holiday with his family.

I assume that this first wave of messages will soon end. But no,
the next day a fresh batch arrives to feast on. It's like having a choc-
olate box with an infinite number of layers; finish one and you just

start another. Soon I'm high on a sympathy rush – and I love it! All this compassion, care and kindness for me! ME! MEEE! Loss is fucking great! It brings a big wonderful warm wave of attention and affirmation. Suddenly you feel totally loved and valued and all those people you once dismissed as narcissistic twats and nasty shits – why, they're now the kindest and most thoughtful people in the world!

All this affirmation and kindness is what we most want and need from the world around us; too bad we have to wait for a loved one to die to get it.

Birth Of A Grief Grump

At first, I'm so grateful even for the corny and the clichéd messages; even the bland, "so sorry for your loss" ones make me teary. I respond to clichés with clichés: "thank you for your kind words/ How thoughtful of you."

But after a day or two of messages, gratitude has given away to grumpitude: I moan and complain about the quality of condolences. A very old friend of mine sends me a text that reads: "Sorry to hear your news. Come have supper x." Is it me or is that a little perfunctory? My friend should have called me or at least written something more than that! That doesn't even qualify as a tweet.

Yes, I know that people mean well and they have busy lives but the brevity of some messages – *Here for you! xx / Thinking of you! Xx Love you! Xx* – now leaves me irritated. It's as if they're discharging a social obligation as quickly as possible, like a hurried thank you note for supper last night. Doesn't the death of a child get a few more words than the average text? If you can't be bothered to say something, I humph, then don't bother!

Life off-line is packed with people who want to offer me their condolences. When I go to pick up my son Dexter from his school there are mums – some I do and some I don't know – who come up and tap me on the shoulder and softly say, "Sorry for your loss." I smile and thank them, but inwardly I sigh. It's only day three of my loss and I'm irritated by the kindness of strangers.

Not exactly a gracious response, is it? But I've become a Grief Grump – and there's no one so hard to please as we Grief Grumps. We're always irritated and exasperated with you lot and how you speak to us. If you don't talk about the dead person we complain about your silence; and if you do say something we complain about what you say – your use of clichés and platitudes. You're too forward. You're too backward in coming forward. You're too evasive and you're too emotional. You're too coy and you're too clingy; you can never win with a Grief Grump.

Rachel Chadwick was a Grief Grump who spoke for many of us. In 2012 her mother died of cancer. In a piece for the *The Daily Mail* she complained about how "inept most people are in dealing with the grief of others." In particular, she singled out the "huggers" who "launch themselves at me uninvited" and the conspicuous sorrow of others that leaves her having to comfort *them*!

I thought I was pretty bad till I read the writer Julian Barnes; he's the preeminent Grief Grump of Great Britain. In his book *Levels of Life* – a part of which deals with the death of his wife the agent Pat Kavanagh – Barnes "tests" his friends on their grief skills. And "some pass" and "some fail." He has dinner with three of them, and when he mentions his wife's name they don't pick up on it. Barnes mentions her name twice more and they ignore him and by implication, her. Barnes concludes, this is not "good manners" but "cowardice". But maybe they just felt awkward or embarrassed? The curious thing is I later heard an interview with Julian Barnes on BBC Radio Four – in conversation with Robert Peston – and he talked about his grief over his wife's death but never once mentioned her name. She was always 'my wife' and never Pat or Pat Kavanagh.

A Short Lesson In The Art Of Condolence

We never know what to say when somebody dies. It feels presumptuous to think we can find the words that are appropriate to the enormity of a death. Our words seem so small, so inadequate for something so big as the loss of a loved one. We long for eloquence, but often settle for the formulaic. And besides, who has time anymore to sit down and write a proper letter of condolence when you can dash off a text in a sec?

But sooner or later everyone has to write something to someone who is in mourning. And you will think: what the hell can I say? But you don't need to say that much. (But please, don't send the perfunctory text. People with class send cards and letters.) The mistake many people make is to think that you have to say something profound or deeply comforting. You don't. A few words about the person who has died – a fond memory or two will do, it can be silly or serious. You're basically giving someone a hug, but with words.

The best message I got was from Kate Morgan, the twenty-two-year-old daughter of my former girlfriend Jane. She wrote to me about being at a party of mine some years ago when I was seeing her mum. (I had asked Kate to babysit Dexter while the party was on.) Jack had asked her if she wanted, "to go outside and smoke a spliff."

Here's what Kate wrote: "I reminded him that I was the baby sitter. It was after turning down Jack's lovely invite to get high that one of your friends spoke to me a little patronisingly. It was really no big deal but Jack literally leapt to my defence in true gent style. 'Don't speak to Kate like that, it's rude.' A few swear words were exchanged (mainly by Jack on my behalf) and I have to say no one has quite defended me like that again. I whispered to him afterwards, 'Thank you.'"

The journalist Katie Glass, who was a friend of Jack's mum, also told me of his kindness and the way he stood up for her, whenever she got into rows with Jack's mum Julie. "Don't speak to Katie that way" he once told his mum. Although she was older than Jack, Katie says that Jack "was oddly protective of me. He went out of his way to make me feel good about myself."

In the wake of his death I kept hearing from people about Jack's "kindness", his "sweetness" and his consideration for other people. It seems he always tried to make people feel good about themselves. He would focus on their problems and rarely talked about his own.

Reading Kate and Katie's words all these years later still fills my eyes with tears. I'd always wanted my son to stand-up for what was right, to be a gentleman and he was – but I was so fixated on the image of The Other grungy-druggy Jack that I couldn't see that Gentleman Jack was standing right before me.

Is there a life lesson in that? If so you'll have to find it yourself. To be honest, I don't know if I can do this positive life-lesson thing for much longer. At the end of the day, at the end of a life what have we to say about it all other than: You die. I die. The people we love die. Shit happens. End of story.

Is that it? Is that the best we can do? No, I can't accept this. The reality of loss deserves something better than this sort of lazy, knee-jerk nihilism. People like me – bookish, metropolitan types – have a cultural and cognitive bias towards the dark view of life. We sneer at the positive thinkers and dismiss them as simpletons in search of that shallowest of pursuits: happiness. Meanwhile, we flaunt our despair as a mark of a superior sensibility. Not me, not anymore.

● ● ●

On my second day back in London, Jack's mum – the journalist Julie Burchill – announced Jack's death on Facebook. "My beloved son Jack Landesman killed himself earlier this week. He is at peace now and in pain no longer and of course I don't believe that life ends with death, so I am lucky. Look after the people you love, as I tried and failed"

I too tried and failed. But then, in the wake of a suicide we all feel like failures. Even the most attentive and loving parent or friend feels that way. We like to think that our love can save a loved one – after all, what have we got that is more powerful than our love?

Nothing. But sometimes the love in our hearts are no match for the demons in their heads.

Death In The Digital Age

At first I thought Julie's message was odd. I mean, who announces the death of their child on Facebook? But maybe I'm the odd one here and this is the new normal. My involvement with social media is minimal. I don't blog, tweet or post on Facebook, though I have a Facebook page.

The experience of death is changing in the digital age; it has lost its entitlements and privileges. Death no longer has any right to privacy and no special status as a unique event in life. Now it's just a nugget of news to feed the insatiable appetite of the chattersphere for novelty. Death may last forever but thanks to social media a death will be forgotten in fifteen seconds.

So there I am bemoaning the trivialising effect of social media when a day after Julie's announcement I see this article heading in *The Independent*: 'Julie Burchill's anti-suicide Facebook plea saved singer Ruby Joy's life.' According to an on-line news site, "Julie Burchill has managed to save the life of a New Zealand woman with her emotional Facebook posts, following the death of her son Jack Landesman."

It seems that a young girl in New Zealand, Ruby Joy, who had been contemplating suicide, had read Julie's posts. Ruby was quoted as saying, "Her raw and honest account of the pain of loss touched me and I realised that my brain had tricked me."

Julie then posted Ruby's message to her on Facebook and the following day Ruby found hundreds of messages of love and support from strangers. "It has shown me that life is precious," said Ruby, "and that lots of people are good".

So much for the trivialisation of death by social media!

• • •

The Daily Mail, *The Guardian*, *The Independent* and *The Daily Telegraph* and even *The Sun* pick up the story of Julie Burchill's son's death by suicide. I'm asked for quotes by newspapers and I say no comment. The *Sunday Times* magazine gets in touch; Julie is writing a piece about Jack for them and would I like to do a five-hundred-word sidebar to accompany her piece? No thanks, I tell them. I tell friends: that's not my style. I'm going to opt for the position of dignified silence. I will not use my kid's death for copy!

Of course that's bullshit. I'm simply not going to play the support act to a headlining Julie. (Jesus, I have some pride left!) I know how petty this must sound, but being petty – and all those bad bits of yourself – are at times like these comforting. They are part of the old you that has got left behind by events. It's kind of reassuring to know that you're still the petty-minded envious hack you were before all this happened. It's like being alone in a foreign country and running into someone you never liked much back home, but now you're glad to run into a familiar face.

• • •

I keep thinking: just go upstairs and get the urn. Don't be afraid. Jack's not going to suddenly pop out as some sort of *Exorcist* like demon, spewing blood and guts, so what are you afraid of?

Jack: Yeah dad, don't be such a pussy. Go get my urn, bitch! It's lonely here in the cupboard. Only joking!

Jack was always saying, "only joking." It was like a nervous tic. He was worried that you might take something he said the wrong way and you'd be offended or he might have hurt your feelings. I must say for a "fucked-up drug fiend" (his words) he had good manners.

The Pills Of Peace

I'd assumed that Jack had killed himself by taking an overdose of Nembutal which is a barbiturate, once commonly prescribed as a sleeping pill. (Nembutal has become the preferred pill of choice for the suicidal because of its reputation for providing a fast and pain-less death.) For months Jack had gone through the complex proce-dures necessary to make an illegal online purchase of this prescrip-tion-only drug. And so when I got the news of his death I thought his little death package must have finally arrived in the post.

I pictured him climbing into bed, wearing his black hoodie and having his laptop by his side…swallowing his pills…closing his eyes…and passing peacefully away as if going to sleep. But this comforting view of his death is shattered when the woman from the coroner's office phones and informs me that Jack was found hanging from the back of his door and she is sorry for my loss.

Jack always said he couldn't face dying alone. (That was another reason I was confident he wouldn't do it.) So from time to time he would turn to me for help.

He'd say: I can't do it on my own. I'm afraid. I don't want to die on my own. Dad, will you keep me company?

No!

Jack wants to go to Dignitas in Switzerland and die there. Would you please go with me?

Nooo!

Jack asks if I will fly with him to Mexico where he can buy Nembutal over the counter and take an overdose. You could just sit with me in the hotel until it's over.

Nooooo!

Jacks asks me for my help to kill himself as if it were a perfectly reasonable request; a favour that any caring father would be happy to oblige.

You know, like…

Dad, can you lend me twenty-quid?

Dad, can I borrow a t-shirt?

Dad, can you help me kill myself?

Jack doesn't understand why I won't help him to die. In saying no to him I think I'm saying: I love you and I care for you. I think I'm being a good dad.

You're being a cunt, says Jack. If I had a terminal disease, you'd help.

I don't believe that you have a terminal disease.

How can you let someone you claim to love suffer like this? It's just so fucking cruel.

Jack, I know things are tough for you but suicide is not the answer.

It is for me!

● ● ●

That comfort I got from my mental picture of his fast and pain free death is instantly destroyed by that call from the coroner. His death is not only a lonely one, it is a violent and ugly thing; more like a murder than the peaceful, soft drift into death. To kill himself like that meant he must have wanted to die so badly. You would think this would help me to grieve, but it only adds to my feeling of numbness. I decide I need to go and see Jack and talk things over; that will do the trick.

A Visit To Jack

I call the funeral home and I tell the manager that I want to see Jack one more time. I want to look him in the face and say goodbye and give him a kiss on his forehead and a little pat on the shoulder the way I used to.

"Mr. Landesman, I don't think that's advisable," says the manager, "The casket is closed. Best remember him as he was."

This is funeral parlour understatement for: believe me mate, you don't want to see your boy in that state!

On arrival I'm shown down a few steps into the 'chapel'. The room is, as you'd expect: quiet, cool, calm. It has a drab dignity to it; a whiff of cheap religiosity and second-hand solemnity that is as synthetic as the alpine air freshener that perfumes the room. On the wall is the face of Jesus. On the floor, a vase of plastic pink flowers. And in the centre of the room, raised about waist height is Jack's coffin.

My first reaction is: *what a cheap looking coffin! Christ almighty, it does look like something from IKEA!* And what's more, it looks too small for Jack. He was about six-two. What did they do to get him in there, cut off his feet? I look at the brass nameplate at the centre of the coffin lid: *they've got his middle name wrong!* It's Tobias, not Tobyn you morons! I'm about to charge off and complain but I hear Jack's voice inside my head: *dad, please don't make a big fuss about the name thing. Who gives a shit? I don't! I think it's funny.*

Jack and I are in the same room. He's in there. In the pine box. My Jack. My dead Jack. If only I could open the lid, lift him out and take him home. I'd make him spaghetti bolognese, which is his favourite. It's hard to know what to say or think or do when you're in a room with your dead child by your side. I want to knock on the coffin top and say, "Jack! I know you're in there! It's me, your useless dad. C'mon rise and shine."

I go and sit on the plastic chair in the corner. My head is bowed and I wait for the torrent of grief to come; but I only manage a little weep. After a few minutes I decided to go home. What can I do?

You can't force grief. So I go over to Jack's coffin and place a kiss where I imagine his head to be.

And I whisper: "Have a good sleep darling" – just like he was a child again and I've tucked him in bed for the night.

• • •

As the weeks go by, my sense of grief inadequacy grows. I carry on as if nothing has shattered the normalcy of my life. I shop. I write. I go to a friend's book launch. Again, I get pissed in Soho. Is this right and proper? Shouldn't I be so overwhelmed by my grief that my ability to function in the world is gone? I want a tsunami of pain and anguish to replace my tepid outpouring of tears.

Why aren't I suffering like a loving dad should? A loving dad like Steve Sorensen author of *Surviving My Son's Suicide: A Father's Perspective*. He writes, "I spent the first three weeks in bed crying everyday, all day until there were no tears left. I couldn't eat or sleep, and I was physically and emotionally ill."

That's Grief

But I'm not physically and emotionally ill. I can eat and sleep. And I don't have dreams starring Jack and I don't have hallucinations featuring Jack, the way some grieving parents do. There's no hollowness in my stomach, no tightness in the chest, breathlessness or any of the other typical symptoms of grief. All that I have is a kind of wobbly-fuzzy feeling.

Something is wrong. Seriously wrong with me. I mean, what sort of dad doesn't really grieve over the death of their child? Maybe I'm not the dad that everyone imagines and admires: the supposedly loving and caring dad, the good dad who, as people keep telling me, shouldn't blame himself for what happened.

I don't even have the right grief look. What's that? Joan Didion in *The Year of Magical Thinking* writes that people "who have lost someone have a certain look. The look is one of extreme vulnerability…(they) look naked because they think themselves invisible."

What is she talking about? I don't think I'm invisible. I don't look vulnerable. There is no such thing as a face of loss; every loss has its own face. I rant to friends about how bad Didion's book is – how humourless and verbose *The Year of Magical Thinking Is* and they look at me as though this is merely my grief talking.

And I'm still making bad taste jokes that nobody finds funny and leaves me feeling guilty. I tell Alice and she sends me a card with a quote from George Bernard Shaw that reads, "Life does not cease to be funny when people die anymore than it ceases to be serious when people laugh."

If I Cry

What makes me feel even worse about my lack of grief is the fact that I'm consumed not by grief but sexual desire. That's right – my libido has gone lunatic on me. All I can think about is having sex. Sex with Alice, friends, old lovers, old girlfriends, strangers, whoever. I can't explain it. All I know is that I feel deeply ashamed at all this feverish fuck-think.

Women – who are close and caring friends of mine – are showing me nothing but simple human kindness with their platonic embraces and their life affirming hugs and what I'm thinking is: *will she fuck me? If I cry will she fuck me?*

What is wrong with men? What is wrong with me?

I confess to close women friends about my sex fever, expecting them to be disgusted with me. I'm disgusted with me and I want that disgust to be affirmed and reinforced by them. I hope they will chastise me with their disgust. I want them to look at me in the eye and say, "get a grip" and "stop acting creepy". I want them to shame me back to being a decent man and a good dad.

But they don't! They say they understand me! They say they get it.

It's a coping mechanism, they say.

No, I insist. It's a copulating mechanism!

They refuse to judge and make me feel ashamed. So I have to try and do that myself. It's too early to be thinking about sex. I feel guilty. I haven't told Alice about this so I feel dishonest. I feel sleazy. I feel terrible.

But most of all I feel like fucking.

All this feverish fuck-think – it's disrespectful to death. It mocks death's gravity and sniggers at its solemnity. It's the illicit hand-job in the back of the dark church; nothing more than trite taboo busting. Infantile and self-indulgent profanity. Death asks us to press the pause button on pleasure and shut-up, sit-still and think, really think about life like an intelligent adult and not a horny hormone driven adolescent.

I should be thinking about my dead son and doing something good for mental health charities but all I want to do is run away and go on some mindless sex-binge. Is that what this crazed carnality of mine is about? Escaping grief?

Jack: Dad this is so gross and disgusting! I beg you, please don't put this stuff in. It makes you sound like such an old sex-mad perv! And a total cunt as well – I mean, who gets horny after their child dies? Man this is some serious sick shit!

Me: Jack, I'm trying to explore a serious and important theme here.

Jack: (laughing) What? Getting laid? That's pathetic, even by your standards!

Me: No! It's about how we try and fit everyone into a fixed idea of what is and isn't appropriate grief. We expect those who are grieving to be these solemn, serious, sexless beings with no feelings other than pain. It's just not so. But it's taboo to talk about it.

Jack: Well, good luck with that. But remember when you get slagged-off and trolled on Twitter for it – I told you so!

• • •

A smart female editor friend of mine told me that all this sex stuff "was really off putting to young women. Best leave it out." I could understand that feeling because like them, I assumed that this sex fever of mine was just a dumb male thing. And then I saw Phoebe

Waller-Bridge's hit TV show *Fleabag* (2018). Consumed by an unprocessed mix of grief and guilt over the death of her best friend, Waller-Bridge's protagonist uses sex to fill the empty hole at the centre of her life. She shows a woman having sex that is devoid of pleasure, of passion, of connection; it is sex as an act of desperation and denial.

Was I in denial too? You can never win with denial. Say you're in denial and well, you're in denial. Say no, I'm not in denial and that's a sign that you're in denial.

So what was this whole sex fever about? I don't know. My guess is I wanted intimacy. I wanted to overcome the numbness I was feeling. I wanted to be wanted. I wanted to be held. I wanted to climb back into the womb. Take your pick because I don't know. Thankfully, the wild bouts of sexual debauchery went on in my head and not my bed. My sexual madness fades after a few weeks, but I'm still left with my grief guilt. What the hell is going on?

• • •

I start reading up on grief and discover all sorts of possible explanations for why I'm not devastated: I'm trying to rush things/ I'm in denial/ I'm delusional/ I'm depressed/ I'm feeling too guilty/ I don't feel guilty enough/ I'm narcissistic/ I'm borderline psychopathic/ I have delayed grief/ I have childhood trauma/ I have attachment issues/ fears of abandonment/ I'm angry/ I'm relieved and I'm just me.

And then one day a terrible thought occurred to me: I do not grieve because I did not love my son.

Is that the explanation? I found this from a diary entry sometime in 2015, "He complains that I don't love him…he's right. I don't. That's my guilty secret…it breaks my heart that it is so but I can't deny it/ I can't pretend that things are otherwise…I hate the kind of person he is."

The reason I was so anxious about signs of real grief was because I wanted to prove to myself and the people who knew Jack that I loved him. If I didn't love him, what kind of father was I? A cold and uncaring fraud! With a father like that, no wonder Jack killed himself.

Everything I read about grief seems to confirm this. The current grief consensus is that the amount of pain you feel is commensurate to the amount of love you had for the dead one. Grief, writes grief expert Julia Samuel, is an "unseen wound that is greater or smaller depending on how much we loved the person who has died." In other words: small wound, small love. No wound, no love.

Things get worse when I look into psychoanalytic literature on grief. In *The New Black* psychotherapist Darian Leader – citing Freud's essay 'Mourning and Melancholia' – writes something that no parent in my position wants to hear. "We'll have difficulties in mourning not because we loved too much…but because our hatred was so powerful."

Is that it? Had my grief got trapped and strangulated in that narrow gap between love and hate?

Parents don't want to talk or write about these contradictory feelings of love and hate, especially about a child who has committed suicide. It's speaking ill of the dead. And for the parent it's hard to escape the thought that maybe if your love had been pure and unconditional, untainted by hate, they'd be alive today.

I Talk It Over With Jack

Me: I fear that the reason I can't grieve properly for you is that something happened to my love for you.

Jack: Thanks dad! That's really nice to know. Cheers!

Me: Look. It's not that simple. Freud says that where there's love, there is always hate.

Jack: *I Man, I can't believe you're still into all that Freud crap and analysis bollocks! Honest dad, it's shit. I know. I did therapy – and it did fuck all for me.*

Me: You made it hard for me to love you. You became this other person, this Other Jack.

Jack: Yeah, well you became this Other Dad. Always losing your temper and shouting at everyone. Anyway, do we have to talk about this stuff? I mean, what's the point? Hello, I'm dead! It's a little bit late in the day for the old dad-son truth and reconciliation routine. You feel me?

Me: Do you have to talk like someone out of *The Wire*?

Jack: Do you have to talk like someone in a therapy session?

Me: I don't know what happened with us. We just drifted so far apart that I lost sight of you. What happened to our love?

Jack: GAY! Only joking!

Me: Jack! Come on, let's just talk. We used to talk a lot in the last couple of years, remember? You'd sit on the sofa and I would be in the armchair and I would try to get you to be more positive about life. All that talk and yet I never told you what you needed to hear: how much I loved you.

Jack: Fuck! This is so embarrassing, I'm out of here. Seriously. It's all good Dad, just chill.

Now For The Bad News

And as if this recognition of the link between love and hate wasn't bad enough, there are psychoanalysts who tell me that on a sub-conscious level I actually wanted my son dead and that when it happens, "At some level we have got what we wanted."

Wait there's more! Not only did we get what we wanted, but there are post-Freudians who argue that mourning is not over until the mourner can acknowledge their delight at the death of the one they loved. *Delight?* Can this be true? Had I had grown so weary of so many years of worry and having this grown-up-fucked-up-child to look after, that I wanted an end to the whole Jack drama?

Here read this. I found it in an old diary of mine from 2014.

"If I'm honest there's a very small part of me that would be relieved if he did kill himself. And not just for the obvious reason that he will at last find some peace – but that I will find some peace. I'm ashamed to say I want my flat back. I want to be able to walk into a room and not smell Jack or see his collection of cups and empty packets of flapjacks and plastic coke bottles."

Of all the terrible thoughts I have about Jack there is one that – if true – is the most terrible and unforgivable thought of them all and it is this: *I wanted that little fucker dead.*

And I got my wish.

6

In Search of Lost Love

If I wanted to break free from my grief paralysis, I assumed I had to discover what happened with Jack and me. Why did things go so wrong? How can the love between a parent and a child that begins as unconditional and absolute, end up so damaged as to appear dead?

I sit at my desk with baby photos of Jack, my old diaries from when Jack was a child, Jack's drawings as a kid and his school reports, trying to summon up the past so that I can knit all these bits and pieces into some sort of coherent story. I'm aware that my desperation to know what happened with Jack might lead to a distortion of the truth.

Of course, the idea that there's a singular Truth out there waiting to be discovered or constructed out of bits of biographical evidence may be the ultimate distortion of the Truth. We are prone to simplification and exaggeration for the sake of narrative coherence – but that coherence is what people who have lost someone to suicide long for. We want a story that makes sense because we think that will ease our suffering. But life is inherently messy and a life that ends in suicide can be so messy it never makes sense.

I still have the small, plastic wrist tag of identification that the hospital put on Jack's wrist right after his birth. I hold it in my hand right now. It's tiny; about an inch in width and an inch in length. I squeeze it between my thumb and my forefinger and it bends into a little mouth like O. I long for it to speak to me. I read the tag inside the plastic casing that's written in blue biro: JACK LANDESMAN. I sniff it and think: through this little hole came Jack's little baby hand; all small and rubbery, with tiny Plasticine fingers.

I wait for its pathos to provoke memories…but nothing comes because it's just a grubby plastic souvenir from a bygone baby-hood. When I die the bits of my life and the mementos of Jack's life will end up in a rubbish bag together.

● ● ●

To tell the story of what happened to Jack and me – and what happened to Jack – I have to go back in time, step into the swamp of memory and stumble around in the dark. I feel like a butterfly collector trying to capture all the facts and fleeting truths I need with a small net full of big holes. Well…here goes.

The birth of a baby is both a mundane fact of life and the nearest most of us ever come to witnessing a miracle. My miracle happened on the 20th March 1986 at 6.35 pm when Jack was born and I was reborn. No longer just a man; I was now a dad.

First came the relief that the baby and his mum were fine and then came that rush of baby bliss. When I held him in my arms he was so small, vulnerable and so in need of my protection and love. Clearly, some evolutionary hard-wiring had been switched on inside of me and I was primed and pumped up to provide it. At that moment as he lay in my arms I was certain that here was a love that was unconditional, invincible and forever.

I used to look back on the days of Jack's childhood in the late 1980s as a time of great happiness for Jack, Julie and me.

Now, I'm not so sure. That's the unique thing about suicide – it not only kills the future you would have had with that person, but it kills the past you had with them as well. Your most treasured certainties don't look so certain anymore and you're left wondering: were they true? Did we have fun together? Did they know how much you loved them?

I used to tell the story of my past like this: once upon a time I was in love with a beautiful and brilliant woman called Julie. We were living the modern metropolitan dream. We had a cool flat in Bloomsbury, hip friends, drugs and more laughs together than any couple in the world. And then we had this beautiful baby and called it Jack. By day we were dutiful parents and by night naughty children. I felt like I had it all; the perfect blend of bourgeois domesticity and bohemian craziness. We were a happy, merry little band of three.

When Jack was a small boy I carried him on my shoulders to the park and we played on the swings and slides together. I blew raspberries on his belly and bounced him on our bed. In his grandparent's garden we'd hunt for bugs beneath rocks together and water the plants – and each other – with a spray hose. On Saturdays I would take him to the Science Museum or the Natural History museum which he loved. There were drowsy afternoons on the sofa watching *Postman Pat, Fireman Sam and Button Moon* together. And then giving him a bath before bedtime and reading a book to him in bed. And then came the demand to read it again. And again. We had such great times together.

And then he dumped me for his mother.

Other Fathers, Other Sons

To gain some perspective on my relationship with Jack I started reading the memoirs of other parents of suicides. I wanted to meet men like me – men who had complex relationships with their damaged sons and problems mourning their death. I did not want to be the odd dad out. I assumed there would be dozens like me. Maybe there were but in my, admittedly limited research, I couldn't find them.

Instead, I found all these loving and caring dads who had these "wonderful" sons who were "handsome" and "brilliant" and blessed with remarkable talents of all kinds. Sons who excelled at sports and attained academic honours or were artistically gifted. These boys were invariably "kind", "helpful", "thoughtful", "loving" and were adored by family members and admired and loved by their peers. Here were sons who often hugged their dads and wrote I-love-you notes to their mums (I'm not joking!) These were sons who were the bright lights that lit up the "lives of everyone around them."

Their sons did not drive them mad or call their dad a "pussy."

Yeah, that's because they were boring wankers!

Shut-up Jack!

• • •

When Jack was alive I was always comparing him to other kids and invariably feeling disappointed; and now that he is dead I'm still comparing him to other kids and feeling disappointed. I know I should be more sceptical about the portraits these fathers present of their sons; these are men caught up in grief, guilt and God knows what, so their memories are bound to be selective.

But I don't care. I'm too far gone in my feelings of envy for these dads and their relationships with their sons. One dad writes that when his son died he lost his "best buddy." They would cook together, go to the cinema together, go to the gym together, go fishing or go hiking together. Another dad writes of his son, "He was my best friend. In those brief 15 years of life, he filled each and every day with joy."

He filled each and every day with joy? Jack, did you hear that! Each and every day!

Jack: Yeah dad, got it the first time! Sorry, but that kid was a total loser! I mean, Jesus, what's he doing hanging-out with his dad every day? That's not normal. That's seriously fucked-up! No wonder he topped himself! He was probably only spending so much time with his dad because he didn't have any other friends.

Me: Jack, for heaven's sake, have a heart.

• • •

Not only did I compare Jack to other kids, but I would compare myself to other dads as well; and I always came second best. The over-anxious mum who wants to be the Perfect Mum is a familiar figure, but the over-anxious man who wants to be Super Dad is less well known.

I saw all these other dads – dads I knew or just dads I'd see in the park with their children – and I envied them. They seemed so close, so connected to their kids. I remember one friend telling me about a trip he took with his son – who was also called Jack – to China. *China*! I couldn't get my Jack to take a trip to the local park with me much less China.

I knew that my dad envy was out of control when, one wet Sunday afternoon, I was watching *Terminator 2: Judgment Day* with Julie and Jack on the sofa. In it, Sarah Connor (Linda Hamilton) is looking at her young son John Connor (Edward Furlong) playing with the cyborg Terminator (Arnold Schwarzenegger) and she goes into this speech about how wonderful the Terminator would be as a dad.

Sarah says, "The Terminator would never stop. It would never leave him. It would never hurt him or say it was too busy to spend time with him. It would always be there. And it would die to protect him. Of all the would-be fathers who came and went over time – this thing, this machine was the only one that measured up. In an insane world it was the sanest choice."

And though rationally I knew I was silly to compare my parenting skills with that of a fictitious Cyberdyne Systems Series T-800 Model 101 Terminator, I couldn't stop myself. And though Julie and Jack said nothing I was convinced their silence signified their agreement with Sarah Connor. In my mind I could see the happy family of Jack, Julie and Terminator on the sofa, consoles in hand, lost in fun.

• • •

Even now after all these years I still compare myself to other dads. I see them on social media – all these pictures of proud beaming dads with their smiling kids at football matches, on holiday, having burgers or at some school event. I watch in wonder and awe at videos of dads who form these little home based pop bands with their kids. Usually there's some three-year-old drummer or a small child who can barely lift up their bass guitar and dad is on lead vocals and guitar – and some of them are really good!

I mentioned my envy to one of these dads who I always see on Facebook with his arms wrapped around the shoulders of his two golden teenage boys and he tells me, "Cosmo. Don't be fooled by those photos. My children can't stand me!"

The Good Dad

So what is a Good Dad? I suspect that most dads don't know how to answer that question – I don't – and yet most dads long to be a Good Dad. That question takes on a whole new urgency in the wake of your child's suicide.

After Jack's death, people kept saying to me, "Don't blame yourself. You were a good dad."

And I would always say: thank you so much for your kind words – *now fuck-off and let me get back to beating myself up for being such a shit dad!*

I didn't say that last bit.

But I thought it, every time.

• • •

People will say you were a good dad because they don't want you to add guilt to the fires of grief. In fact, they don't know if you were actually a good or bad dad or even a bit of both. But you know, don't you? Because you've put yourself on trial and you are your own prosecutor, defender, jury, judge and executioner; and you've found yourself guilty. Guilty of what? Guilty of everything: of negligence, of failing in your duty of care, of not being loving enough, of letting your child down. (And don't forget the rest of your now devastated family that you failed.) That time you shouted at your child over something silly – guilty! – and the time you didn't turn up for the school play because of work – guilty! And you're guilty of this and guilty of that and guilty of just being a big fucking useless crap dad who couldn't save his child! That's right! The one thing you had to do, the one supreme challenge you faced as a man and a dad – you couldn't do it. And that's why your child is dead. And when all those nice, well-intentioned people say to you in that soft caring voice; don't blame yourself you were a good dad, you know the truth don't you?

• • •

Was there anything more I could have done to save Jack? Only about a million-and-one things. But there's no guarantee that a million-and-one things would have saved him. You might be wondering: did this guy ever try and do anything practically to help his son? It's a fair question.

I'd say to him: *Jack why don't you . . .*

Eat proper food. You can't live on sandwiches and fizzy drinks.

Try to do a bit of exercise, you'll feel better. I promise.

Try mindfulness, it really works!

Stop taking drugs – they're destroying your mind! Go to NA meetings. Just try one. Please!

Get retraining for a better job – you need to make a living.

Why not move to a different country, get a fresh start? Ok, that's a bit ambitious. Forget it!

Don't come off your medication – it makes you more depressed!

Don't always be so negative. You need to think more positively.

Go back into therapy and stay in therapy for at least a year.

Do some voluntary work. It will help you get back into work.

Get a girlfriend.

Get a dog.

Get a band together.

Get a life!

And Jack would always respond with either:

1   I tried that. It didn't work.

2   What's the point?

3   My brain is broken.

4   The old me is dead.

Doing Dad And Son Things Together

When Jack was a toddler we did tons of things together and then around the age of ten he just wanted to be with his mum. I wanted us to go off to the local park and do sporty dad-son things together like play catch and football. I'd pictured us having hours of exhausting, sweaty fun. So I bought us a football. And an American football. And a basketball. And an American baseball (and bat) and a cricket bat and ball. But Jack had no interest in afternoons in the park, kicking, hitting or catching any kind of ball.

"Balls are boring!" declared Jack.

Ok, I thought, so Jack is not sporty. That's fine. Everyone is different. I'll find something else we can do together. But he hated being dragged around art galleries and places of historical interest never interested Jack. And he wasn't interested in the magic of art or the wonders of science anymore. Dinosaurs were now dull and *Postman Pat* was for kids. His curiosity about the world collapsed and he became interested in one thing only: video games.

None of the Dad-Son things I suggested we do together could ever compete with the joy of staying indoors on a sunny afternoon and playing *Super Mario Brothers* or *Sonic the Hedgehog* with his mum. (She actually loved all that stuff). The two of them would sit on our big leather sofa, game consoles in hand, staring at the television screen, squealing with delight or shrieking with disappointment. Together they were wrapped up in their own impenetrable cocoon; mother and child bonded in video game bliss.

I didn't know it at the time but a new era of childhood was in the making, one in which the screen would be the centre of a child's focus; the dominant provider of play and pleasure. The childhood rooted in the world outside the security of the family home was being left behind. In this new childhood of the screen, what use was it to be a fun dad? I couldn't compete with the endless and engrossing pleasure of the video games of Jack's youth. How quaint this sounds in the age of the iPhone. I sound like some old duffer complaining about some new-fangled invention called the wireless.

Now I wonder: why didn't I just join in with Jack and his mum and play video games too? At least give them a go? Because I thought I was too damn superior for that sort of "mind-rot." I, like many educated middle-class parents at the time, assumed that video games turned children into "video morons." I wanted to do culturally uplifting things and outdoors things with my son and not just sit there, passively spellbound before a screen.

I had this fixed idea of what a good childhood should be. It was the pre-internet childhood of playing football in the street with your friends until it got dark; it was zooming around on your bike miles from home with the wind in your face, breathing in that first whoosh of freedom. It was going on a number 19 bus and wandering around the West End, staring in wonder at all the guitars on display in the guitar shops of Denmark Street.

In other words, the childhood I kept trying to push Jack into was mine.

I did make sporadic attempts at tempting him away from his beloved video games. It would be one of those sunny afternoons that are perfect for a dad and son kickabout in the local park. I'd come bouncing into the living room, football in hand and say, "Come on Jack, it's a beautiful day outside. Let's go to the park and have a kickabout – and we can get some ice-cream."

But no. Not even the bribe of one of those Mr. Whippy Ice creams you get from an Ice Cream van – with the extra inducement of a Cadbury's Flake and a splash of strawberry syrup – could tempt him to come out and play with me. Jack just sat by his mother's side, unwilling to move his eyes away from the screen, unwilling even to turn his head and address me face to face. He'd sit transfixed before the screen, holding the sacred console in his hands and grunt, "No thanks!" over his shoulder like a piece of litter thrown from a speeding car. And then he'd disappear back down the plug-hole of Super Mario world with his mum for the rest of the afternoon.

Mum Vs Me

Was I jealous of their relationship? You bet. Jack and Julie had so much fun together, they were more like mates than mother and child. Their special bond was recognised by Jack when he was seven or eight, when he said to Julie, "I don't need a brother or sister – I've got you! You're my mum and sister too."

And that's the way she saw it. In her *Sunday Times* article, written after his death, Julie wrote: "Jack and I were devoted to each other and I was his playmate as well as his protector; we played video games together deep in the night and we romped at theme parks for hours on end."

In her piece there's no reference to my relationship with Jack. That's understandable because that's how she saw things: it was all about Jack and Julie. Any man in my position would have ended up a footnote in their story. She once told me she loved him more than any man in her life (me included) – and given that, she was unlikely to want to share his affection with anyone, including his dad.

When it came to loving and being loved, there was an element of playground power politics about her divide and conquer approach. Julie had to be number one; the Queen of Hearts; the adored girl everyone wanted to be best friends with. And Julie knew how to seduce everyone. Whoever took her fancy – men, women, children – Julie would love bomb them into adoration. She used the power of her celebrity, her charm and her humour to enchant her victim. And under her spell her new conquest had the thrilling illusion that they were Julie's new best friend forever.

She had one other gift that was hard to resist: she knew how to have fun. Doesn't everyone? Maybe, but her fun was more fun than other people's fun. She knew how to take an ordinary good time, change gears, alter the chemistry, pump up the volume, order another round, put out another line so that the fun you were having with her was faster and more intense than with other people. By the velocity of her excess she'd lift you up – levitation through intoxication – and for a moment you felt like you had broken through the gravitational pull of your prosaic life and personality. Around Julie you thought you were bigger and better – more fun, funnier, smarter, sexier – than ever before. It was a lovely feeling – until she dumped you for her next new best friend.

Julie's Culture War

You can see why a young boy like Jack loved being with her; she was the perfect playmate. With Julie there was none of that middle-class concern with finding culturally uplifting activities for their little darlings. No boring trips to museums, weary wanderings around art galleries and bum numbing nights at the theatre. Her attitude was: *fuck your precious Picasso and shit on Shakespeare too while you're at it!* No normal kid wants to do all that bollocks when there are theme park rides, new video worlds to explore and ice lollies galore in the fridge! Jack's mum was an old-fashioned, hedonistic working-class girl who believed that a lot of what you fancied did you good. She had a child's greedy compulsion for immediate guilt-free gratification; and an adult's income to grab it all and gobble it down fast. What man, what dad could compete with that?

And then one day in May 1995 that warm, wonderful bliss inflated bubble that Jack lived in with his mum suddenly burst; Julie decided that our marriage was over.

• • •

So What's Life Lesson Number Three?
Don't Marry Beautiful, Brilliant, Crazy, Heart-Breaking Women Like The Young Julie Burchill?

No, but it's worth keeping in mind. Life Lesson Three is: *Keep an Open Mind*. If only I had tried to join in with the whole video game thing, I could have been on that sofa with Jack and Julie and we could have been happy video morons together! But no, I had to follow my fixed and antiquated idea of what fathers and sons and families did together. I had excluded myself from the Julie and Jack gang – but then, I'm not so sure they would have let me join their gang in the first place.

• • •

I keep imagining that once I go and get the urn I will have Jack back in my life, and then I think: who am I kidding? That is just the fanciful imaginings of a sad and guilt-ridden dad. The fact is: Jack is gone and he ain't coming back. And nothing I say or do – write a book, raise money for mental health charities or bring out the urn – is going to change that. Everyone who has experienced loss knows that the only thing that you really want is the one thing you can't have: them. So why bother with anything else?

Jack: Hey dude, don't be so negative – as you used to say to me all the time! Go work for a charity. Get a dog. Join a band. Try therapy. Write a novel. Learn to cook. I thought you were into all this life after loss bollocks? You can change your life if you want to – remember that one? Not so positive now are we pal!

Me: Ok, point taken.

Jack: *But seriously dad, you need to do something with your life. Don't give up and go back to wallowing in misery. It's not your style. You're a good writer. You should write.*

Me: Really? Did you ever read any of my stuff?

Jack: *Yeah, well…no, not much. I liked your film reviews, but all that dating stuff was pretty fucking embarrassing! I mean no kid wants to read that sort of thing.*

Me: Well, that's a compliment – of sorts and I think I'll take your advice and stay positive and keep going.

7

Father and Son Together, At Last!

I don't really want to go into the details of the end of my marriage to Julie. Just let me say that after ten years together Julie had grown bored with me and fallen in love with someone else. It happens. Our break-up wasn't easy on Jack – but divorce is rarely easy on kids or their parents. We did the classic, we-both-love-you and nothing-is-going-to-change speech that divorcing parents always make to their children. No doubt this set speech makes parents feel better, but I suspect it provides little comfort for children. They're not convinced by it because they intuitively know that everything has changed. Life with mum and dad as they knew and loved and needed is over. That comforting certainty has collapsed.

In the days that followed I told myself I had to man-up for Jack's sake, but it was also for my sake. She was gone from the family home but not his life. There was no time for sorrow and self-pity – however tempting they were. My main task was helping Jack to adjust to this big scary change by creating a sense of continuity. I did all the things she used to do for him: cooking, cleaning, preparing his packed lunch for school and even – on occasion – playing video games.

I was happy doing these things because they provided the distraction from the sadness I felt and it would, hopefully, bring me closer to Jack. I told Jack about a hundred times a day that I loved him. That his mother loved him. That we loved him. But Jack didn't want these declarations of love; he wanted his family back together.

• • •

There was now a new noise that came into our life – it was the silence of her absence. Her fussing over him. Her sending me off to the shops for her supplies. Her on the phone to one of her girlfriends talking about nothing in particular for hours in that squeaky Minnie Mouse voice of hers. Or her just making that little soft puff of a lip smack she'd make, blotting her freshly painted lips against a tissue.

It was a heavy silence, because neither one of us would mention it. And it was loudest when we sat down to dinner. I would come in with a meal I knew Jack loved – like chicken dinosaurs and chips – and talk about the wonderful desert that was to follow – "it's your favourite!" and what "wonderful thing!" we could watch on TV after dinner.

But after a bit of chat about school and his friends we'd fall into a silence, both sitting at the dinner table thinking the same thing: *I wish she were here.* To keep the silence and the sadness at bay we'd watch episodes of *The Simpsons* as we ate. In those days you got two episodes in a row, which was just what we needed.

The toughest challenge I faced in those early days after her departure was me trying to hide my sadness from Jack. The toughest challenge Jack faced was hiding his sadness from me. I kept smiling and acting in a relentlessly cheerful way like some crazed bluecoat at a holiday camp insisting we're gonna have FUN! FUN! FUN! together. And Jack? Recently I found this, from June 28, 1995. I wrote a letter to Jack to be read when he was older and it said: "Since Julie left I know that things haven't been easy for you.

But you have handled the situation with such bravery – never moaning about her absence and always considerate about my feelings whenever you have gone to stay with her."

He was always very careful not to show any favouritism towards either Julie or me. The strain of that became visible when he developed a series of nervous facial tics and head twitches.

Watching him twitch away I'd put my hand on his shoulder and say: Are you ok Jack?

"Yeah yeah. It's all good," he'd insist. But his little twitchy face told a very different story.

• • •

Jack was seeing his mum one or two nights a week and staying with her on the weekends. When I arrived at her place to pick Jack up and take him home he looked flushed with fun and was excited to show me some new toy he'd been given and he'd talk excitedly about something he and Julie had watched on TV.

I always felt like I was dragging him away from a great kid's party back to the drab Dickensian workhouse that was our home. Clearly, Julie had lost none of her capacity to show a boy a great time. They'd go together for weekend trips to Brighton. During one of their visits I got a card from Jack that read:

Dear Cosmo,

Here I am in Brighton, I am really enjoying myself. I miss you a lot. The Brighton Thistle is great! They have Sky movies, The Movie channel, Sky Movies Gold and Sky One (which means *The Simpsons*, *Robocop* and *Cops*!) Today is Friday and *The Pelican Brief* is on tonight (plus a whole bunch of cool horror movies!) Love you, see you soon!

Love

Jack xxxx

It was great that Jack and his mum were having fun like the old days – at least, that's what I kept telling myself every time an attack of jealousy struck. And besides, I reasoned, why should I be jealous of the fun he has with her? He has fun with me too.

Doesn't he?

• • •

A year after Jack's death I asked his good buddy Poria if Jack ever talked about having fun with me. ("Go on, be totally honest," I said.) Poria looked awkward. He didn't know what to say. How do you tell a grieving dad that their dead son never had any fun with them? Then suddenly his face lit up, "Oh yeah," he said, "Jack liked going to the Trocadero with you."

We used to go there on Saturday mornings. Located in Piccadilly Circus it was like the department store version of your typical small Fun Arcade. It had floors of every mechanised pleasure machine imaginable: shooting games, car racing games, dodgems, dancing games, punching games, pinball, virtual football, hit the mole and a whole floor of wall to wall video games. Jack would play his beloved Mortal Combat for hours – by his side I stood reading the *Guardian*, trying to ignore the grunts and groans that climaxed into the final cry of: "FINISH HIM!"

• • •

With his mum gone from the family home, here was my chance to have my son to myself and be the dad I'd always dreamt of being. Who was this mythical Good Dad of my imagination?

He was a strong and silent dad. A dad who was rather straight and a bit dull perhaps, a touch distant, but he was dependable and decent and he made you feel safe and secure. My fantasy dad knew how to fix everything from the leak in the loo to the problems in your life.

For all his crazy boho ways, my dad was also your traditional dad who taught me how to ride a bike, drive a car, shave, wear a suit and fix things around the house. (When I was older he taught me how to mix the perfect martini.) I would watch him in awe as he showed me how to strip down a piece of electrical flex, twist the copper endings to a point and explain the mystery of where the neutral, earth and live wires went. With his small, yellow, screwdriver – the one with the little red top – in his bony fingers, he seemed to me like some brilliant surgeon conducting a delicate operation with total calm and confidence. "There you go," he'd say and voila: there'd be light.

So when it was my turn to be a dad I thought it was my dad's duty to teach all these things to my son. Isn't that what dads are meant to do? I used to imagine Jack as my eager, teenage assistant, following me around the house, carrying my toolbox and watching in awe at my magical acts of DIY. The fact that I was totally use-less at DIY – often causing destruction that required expert help to repair – did nothing to stop this crazy fantasy.

But Jack didn't see the necessity of learning to rewire a light or change a fuse. He didn't need me to show him how to fix a bike puncture because he never used the bike I'd bought him. (And thank God for that, as I had no idea how to fix a bike puncture. Remember this was a pre-Google age.) I didn't teach him to shave. Or how to drive a car. And I never taught him how to mix a good martini. (I was looking forward to that one.) I think it's fair to say that my attempt to teach my son essential life skills ended in total failure. The thing is, he didn't teach himself either.

But if I couldn't teach Jack anything – what was the point of me as a father? He could find love, money and laughs from his mum. When I said this to a girlfriend she laughed. "Jesus Cosmo. You're the only dad in the world who has an existential crisis because you didn't teach your son how to mix a martini!"

I think I tried so hard to be a great Dad because I wanted Jack to like me. Why was his approval so important to me? After all, my dad's generation of dads didn't worry about being a good or bad dad; they just got on with their lives as dads. We wanted our dads to approve of us; now we want our children to approve of us dads. I think Jack's approval was so important to me because if I had his love and admiration, I could love and approve of myself.

Dreams Of A Normal Dad

In some ways my dad was completely different from my dream dad. Born in the USA, he had been a Greenwich Village beatnik in the 1950s and after moving the family to London he and my mother went all hippie in the 60s. His dope-taking-open-marriage-lifestyle was a source of incredible embarrassment to me in my early teens. I wanted to have what I called at the time a "normal" dad i.e. the quiet dad who didn't hog the social limelight but stood in the background of your life.

Back then I was convinced that all my friends had normal dads while I alone had – and suffered – the weirdo dad. I saw these other dads on parent's day at school and they looked normal and they acted normal. My dad looked weird – arriving at school in his flowerily bell-bottom trousers, purple shirt, shades, long hair, love beads and purple toe nails poking through his sandals. The spectacle of my father – along with my equally flamboyant mother passing through the school gates – caused one of my class mates to cry out in astonishment: *"Fuck me, the Martians have landed!"*

So for Jack's sake I was determined to be the kind of normal dad I had longed for when I was young. When I took him to school I was careful about what I wore – nice, conservative suits – and not act in a way that would draw attention to myself or him. And yet he still found my presence anywhere near the school gate a source of embarrassment.

And I played at being a proper normal dad. I checked on Jack's homework and demanded rewrites when the work wasn't up to scratch. I gave him little normal dad lectures on the need for self-discipline and putting effort into what ever he did and the importance of a tidy room – stuff my dad dismissed as "total bull-shit". Now I realise that I was not being the dad that Jack needed – I was being the dad I needed when I was Jack's age.

But for all his freaky bohemian ways my dad was a fun dad. He knew how to make life fun for my brother Miles and me. Instead of dragging us off to museums and "places of historical interest", he drove us to rock festivals, underground happenings, avant-garde movies at London's Arts Lab and celebrity packed parties.

And I wanted to be a fun dad for Jack and for us to do fun dad-son things together. And now with Julie gone from the family home, here was my chance. I had lost a wife, but gained a son.

The trouble was, there was nothing fun about my approach to having fun. I couldn't just do silly things with Jack – play board games, cook crazy things or even play video games. No, I had to have good, instructive, proper Dad & Son fun. At the top of my list was going to the park and playing catch. I knew that Jack found balls "boring" but I explained that away by telling myself that he'd never really given it a go and with a gentle nudge he'd discover the simple pleasure of a sunny afternoon in the park throwing a ball back and forth with his dad – just like I had done with my dad when I was a boy. We just played catch for ages, lost in the easy rhythm and soothing repetition of throw-catch-throw-catch.

There was only one problem: Jack, I discovered, didn't know how to catch a ball. My son was eleven and he couldn't catch a ball! I was shocked! All boys and girls know how to catch a ball. Even nerdy, non-sporty types of boys know how to catch a ball. It didn't matter if Jack never wanted to catch or touch a ball again in his life. Fine. But I felt that I was failing in my parental duty to equip him with one of the basic life skills – like reading, riding a bike, swimming – if he should never learn how to catch a ball.

And so against his will I began to drag him off to the local park for ball catching lessons; I never saw Jack look so miserable. In response to his groans of protest I was resolute: "You're going to learn to catch a ball, whether you like it or not!"

Eventually, after much suffering, Jack learned to catch a ball. (But we never played catch in the park.) And eventually, I learned what an insane dad I was.

But by then it was too late.

We Go On Holiday

I decided we'd drive down to Dorset and have our first Dad-Son holiday staying together in a lovely cottage an ex-girlfriend lent me. One day we went fishing at a nearby fish farm. Ah, fishing with my son. Here at last was a real dad-son activity! Even Jack would have to admit that this was going to be so much better than sitting indoors on a sunny day watching mind-rotting video games.

Everything was going well at the fish farm, until Jack caught a fish and reeled it in. Seeing the poor fish at the end of the line caused Jack to drop his fishing rod and we both watched the fish flip-flopping on the wooden dock. "Do something dad!" Jack cried.

Here was my chance to be a proper dad. All I had to do was take the fish in one hand and with the other, extract the hook from its mouth and then kill it – or put it back in the water. Simple. But I was scared to go near it, scared to touch it. And my inability to do what-a-dad's-gotta-do left me feeling embarrassed in front of Jack and all the other dads with their kids. My dad inadequacy was now on public display. My fellow anglers began to watch the mini-drama starring the useless dad, the distressed son and the defiant fish.

Jack kept begging me to do something and I kept insisting that the fish will stop flapping about in just a second but that bloody fish kept doing its gravity-defying Olga Korbut like display of flips, twists and spins.

Eventually, one of the other dads took pity on me and said, "Here, let me give you a hand mate." And with one smooth move he picked up the fish, took the hook from its mouth, hit its head on the ground and handed me the dead fish.

By now Jack was on the verge of tears and I was so ashamed we snuck back to our cottage. I hoped to make up for the fish fiasco by giving Jack a lesson in how to cook a fish – but coming from a fish farm our catch was so tasteless as to be inedible.

"I know, lets make a fire!" I said. Boys love making fires, I thought. Jack was excited by the prospect – but the wood we gathered was too damp to catch fire. Neither one of us said it, but we both wished we could end our holiday and just go home. A day later we admitted defeat and did just that.

8

The Funeral

I'd made the funeral arrangements for my father's death in January 2011 and six months later for my mother. Now four years later, here I was arranging the funeral of my son. Burying my parents had been emotionally easy because they had both enjoyed rich and happy lives. When they died my dad had been ninety-one, bedridden and with Alzheimer's. My mother was seventy-nine and was losing her eyesight and she ached all over. It was their time to go.

But I can find nothing consoling in Jack's death. For his mum there's comfort in the idea that at last Jack has found peace; but not for me. There is not only the emotional hurt but a sense that something unnatural had occurred because the normal sequence of family life had been shattered by his death. Our children are meant to bury us; we don't bury them.

I email Julie about the funeral and she's happy for me to make the arrangements and sends suggestions for songs to be played at the service. I've decided to keep his funeral simple. I will give the main eulogy. His mum might want to say something. A couple of his friends will pay tributes. My friend Evie will sing *Fire and Rain* and that's it. A fancy farewell wouldn't be appropriate for Jack. So no flowers. No fuss. No celebratory wake afterwards. I will just invite family and close friends to come to the St. Marylebone Crematorium at 12pm and say goodbye.

What I need now is a nice photo of Jack for the service programme. There are plenty of photos of Jack looking happy as a toddler, but none as an adolescent or an adult. Looking through my
collection of Jack photographs the choice is between Gloomy Jack,
Depressed Jack and Please-Don't-Take-My-Fucking-Photo Jack.
I just want one photo of a happy Jack. Every picture, they say, tells a
story. And the absence of a picture tells a story too.

What makes Jack's death extra sad was that though his life had
been short – he was twenty-nine when he died – it had not been
a sweet one. But nor was it a life devoid of any happiness as Jack
claimed. He once wrote: "Even before this shit happened to me
I wasn't able to take pleasure in the things that most people do.
I remember the first time I went to a gig, my first girlfriend, stuff that
make most people genuinely happy but with me they've always
been dominated by anxiety, fear or just a total lack of emotion.
My mind has constantly found ways to undermine every source of
happiness in my life."

This is the story Jack told himself to make sense of his life.
But like most of the stories we tell ourselves to make sense of our
lives, this one was not rooted in reason and supported by facts.
His life was not unmitigated "shit"; it just looked that way to Jack.
This was a work of fiction created by a depressed and distressed
mind that Jack took for fact.

Life Lesson Number Four: *Don't Believe The Stories You Tell Yourself*

The most unreliable narrator of them all is that voice inside
your head. It's a liar. A con-artist. A cheat. And sometimes a killer.

It's common to say that great fiction can change lives, but the fictions we tell ourselves can end them as well. This is storytelling at its most lethal. I suspect that had Jack been able to create an alternative story to tell himself about his life – one that was more positive, one with hope – then he might be alive today. But there comes a point when the depressed mind goes into lock down mode and refuses to allow alternative and more hopeful narratives a chance to take root and grow into reality. For the suicidal individual, this is often the point of no return.

• • •

My prayers are answered! The happy photo of Jack I want suddenly appears on Facebook courtesy of a mutual friend, Kathy Best. His hair is long and greasy and he has a bit of a scruffy beard, but he's smiling a big grin of a smile – against a blue sky – and this makes me smile. Jack actually looks happy! Happy Jack! Who would have thought it? But then I wonder: is this a moment of genuine Jack happiness or was he just high on drugs? Is smiling Jack just a stoned Jack? Anyway, I've got my photo of Jack I can use. Now all I have to do is figure out what the hell I'm going to say at his funeral. I don't want to stand there before all those people and lie and I don't want to tell the truth. What am I supposed to say: Umm…it was complicated? With Jack's death I got what I subconsciously wanted?

I get the service programmes back from the printers and they look really good. The whole thing is going to be great. Jack will have his mum, me and people who love him to say goodbye. No need to worry now. What could possibly go wrong?

And then on the day before the funeral this appears on Facebook from his mum: "With sorrow I have to announce that I cannot attend the funeral of my son tomorrow. Am in extraordinary pain. Thank you so much to everyone who made Jack's life better. I will be mourning my boy in my own way and for a long time."

I reacted to this with a wave of anger – *how could she?* She'd warned me a few days earlier that her legs had given way and was barely able to walk. Ok, I thought, so crawl. Get on your knees and crawl. Or get a wheelchair – just be there for him.

And then I was sorry and full of regret that I had reacted that way. How sanctimonious and unfeeling of me! Not only was I demanding I grieve in a certain way, I was demanding his mother do the same thing too. I realised that she couldn't come to his funeral, not because of her legs – but because of her broken heart. It was the depth of her love and the agony of her grief that wouldn't let her go. She just could not face seeing her beloved boy in the box.

I knew that Jack wouldn't have cared that she was absent. He had no time for the rites and rituals of life or death; he didn't go to the funeral of my parents or to my wedding to my second wife Maxine. He would have defended Julie's decision with a shrug of his shoulders, saying: "It's no big deal." He was protective of her, till the end. And the really sad thing is he would have meant it. I can hear him saying it loud and clear: "It's all good, dad. It's all good. Chill."

On the day of the funeral I'm having anxious thoughts: will Jack get bums on seats? The chapel can accommodate 148 sitting down, but I've only invited around fifty people. Will any of them come? I worry about my performance. Will I be able to greet people and give the eulogy without breaking down? (I also worry that I won't break down and I'll appear cold and uncaring.) Funeral decorum demands that when giving your eulogy you keep it together and kind of fall apart at the same time. I worry about the songs I've chosen and the performers. Is it a good idea to have my other son Dexter read a poem he has written for Jack or is that too corny? Will everyone like it? Will they like me? I rebuke myself: for heaven's sake, it's a funeral – not the opening night of a West End musical!

● ● ●

I've always thought that a funeral should have grey skies shedding big grim tears of rain, but Jack gets sunshine and a blue sky. It's as if God wants to have the last laugh and show him how beautiful life can be.

And Jack gets a good turn out. The funeral crowd is a mix of my friends and his. Mine are the grown-up ones with their suits and ties and formal dresses. They look awkward in black, as if they are having to wear itchy school uniforms on a hot day. Jack's people are the pale and pierced ones with black hair; they're people who always wear black. But today they resemble Goths trying to look respectable. Given the lovely weather and this socially mixed crowd, this could be Jack's wedding instead of his funeral.

I am surprised – and pleased – by the number of Jack's women friends that turn up. Many of them strike me as outsiders; women who don't fit conventional notions of beauty or being a woman, and what's more they don't care. Women who are often dismissed by men as "fat" or "frumpy" or too this and not enough of that. I can hear my father's voice inside my head as he utters from the corner of his mouth, "Look at all these ugly broads – no wonder Jack killed himself!"

Jack would have hated that sort of talk. I know what he would have said: *That's so fucking disrespectful! Your dad's a cunt.* Although Jack indulged in all that white-boy-gangsta talk of 'ho's' and 'bitches' he always did it in that self-conscious, ironic way of young white guys who know it's silly to try and talk that way.

Not Like Other Boys

The best tribute I heard about Jack came after the funeral from Annabel, a girl Jack had played in a band with. She told me that one of the things that she loved about him was that he never made her feel bad about the way she looked. They had met on an online dating site – Plenty of Fish – and she spotted straight away that he was different from other boys his age.

"He wasn't a typical guy," says Annabel. "He was really funny and really nice to me. He didn't act like all he wanted to do was sleep with me. Jack was like, 'How's your day?' He wanted to know about me. On that site it was like, 'Hey, send me a naked photo!' It was unusual for someone to ask about me about myself."

Eventually Jack suggested they meet in Camden Town. "I was nervous because I've always been a big girl," says Annabel, "and I worried he might think: God, you're much fatter than in your photo! I spent ten minutes explaining to him about my measurements and he was like, 'No man shut-up! I don't care about that shit!'"

He really didn't. And he didn't care about all that other stuff that goes with being a young man; the need to find affirmation or status in sexual conquest, the way I did at his age. He never boasted about getting laid or talked about having a hot date. We never talked about love and sex – at least to me – except once when he expressed his regret at having screwed-up a relationship with a woman he loved. "I'm such a fucking idiot," he said in despair. I got the feeling he wanted friendship with women – and if love and sex followed that was a bonus.

• • •

Throughout the service I keep thinking: I wish Jack were here. (And of course he was; stuffed into that cheapo coffin to the side of the lectern.) He'd see just how loved he was and watch the tears of friends and family. But the really sad thing is this: *it wouldn't have made any difference.*

Me: Would it Jack?

Jack: No. But it's nice and stuff that people came. I appreciate it, I do. I just don't really…care. Sorry. You shouldn't have gone to all this hassle. I mean, you could have just cremated my sorry ass and dumped the ashes down the toilet! It wouldn't really make any difference.

Me: It would to me Jack. It would to me.

• • •

I give the eulogy and judging by the flow of tears it goes down well. I don't say anything about our troubled relationship. What can I say? I talk about Jack's drug use and his suicide, which I later learn is not usually mentioned at funerals. I say that his mind played "terrible tricks" on him – told him that he was "worthless" and the only thing he could do was kill himself.

And then I say: "But my mind played terrible tricks on me," and I could feel the tears welling up in my eyes. I pause. I take a deep breath and say, "I lost something precious. I lost sight of you. That mind of mine did the most awful trick; it hid the lovable you from me."

I say that thanks to the shared memories and comments from all of you here today I feel that I've got my boy back. I feel a bit of a fraud for saying it – for it's more of a work in progress than an accomplished fact. Slowly I'm seeing lovely things about Jack that I haven't seen in years; things that got eclipsed by my concept of The Other Jack.

My friend Evie Vine sings James Taylor's *Fire and Rain* and I cry and so does everyone else. Two of Jack's closest friends – Poria and one-time girlfriend Bianca Flump – give wonderful tributes and Dexter reads his poem. And then comes the final bit at the end where we all sit in silence for a few minutes to reflect on Jack. I get up and go to his coffin and give it a farewell pat. "Goodbye my darling boy," I say, and I press a red button. I can hear the gentle whirl of wheels in motion and the coffin starts to move towards that mystery space beyond the red velvet curtains, to begin its journey to the fires of the furnace.

A Weekend Away

After the funeral Alice whisks me away to a luxury hotel/spa in the countryside for the weekend. What a nice surprise and just what I need! I'm so happy to be having a mini-break from Jack and most of all me. We swim. We hit the sauna. We have massages. We watch movies. And then a strange thought for someone who has just lost a son strikes: I am a lucky man.

The next morning, we come down to breakfast and there's Jack's face staring from the cover of *The Sunday Times* magazine. Beneath a picture of him looking rather serene the strapline reads: "Julie Burchill mourns her son Jack." It seems that everyone in the room is reading Julie's story! (Fuck! Doesn't anyone read the *Observer*?) Even Alice starts reading Julie's piece.

"Traitor!" I mutter.

I can't face reading it. So I watch others reading it. It's odd seeing people flick through the pages of my son's life story – including photos of him and me together – with that casual flick-fo-cus-forget semi-concentration people employ with Sunday papers at the breakfast table. I suggest to Alice we have breakfast some-where else. We get up and leave.

But the day is ruined. Even though Alice has hidden Julie's piece from view, it follows me around. I can hear it calling out to me in a soft, teasing Julie voice: *c'mon...you know you want to read me! You want to see if I'm any good...see if I'm better than the piece you would have written. C'mon big boy, don't be afraid!*

So I read the bloody thing.

And weep.

Soon after her piece appears *The Independent* asks if they can reprint my funeral eulogy for Jack. (Julie posted a copy of it I sent her, on her Facebook page.) I agree immediately, but tell commissioning editor Tim Willis I don't want to give my fee to some mental health charity or make a big song and dance about how I'm doing it to raise awareness of the issue of suicide. Fuck that. I want applause. I want people to think I'm a good writer and this is a great piece.

A few days later Terence Blacker in *The Independent* writes an interesting piece about why we like to wallow in the grief of other people. He calls Julie's piece, "brilliant" and "gut wrenching" and "fearless", while my piece is just a "moving eulogy." But hey, all funeral eulogies are moving!

What's more, Julie's piece raises lots of money for mental health charities. "It's well into five figures," she says on Facebook. The only thing my piece raises is praise for my ravenous ego.

But Terrence Blacker is right when he writes about Julie's piece, "There was an element of showing-off here." This is confirmed by a Facebook posting of Julie's where she thanks her fans: "I'm just so knocked out by your amazing responses to my tribute to my boy."

As Blacker points out, all writers – including him – show-off and crave applause and I'm no different. For the real writer all of life is copy – and so too is death.

9

Jack's Things

Now that Jack has been buried, it's time to go and collect his things from his bedroom in Harrow. I'm hoping that the reality of his room, seeing his Jack things, seeing the Jack door that he hung himself from will finally trigger that great purge of grief I long for.

Since his death I've avoided thinking about what went on in that small white room of Jack's during the minutes leading up to his suicide and the hours afterwards. Every time I'm tempted an inner alarm goes off that says: *don't go there*!

And now I'm going there. Into the room. Into the Jack death room.

• • •

Why did Jack choose to live on a quiet residential street in the middle of nowhere? No reason. It was just the first place he spotted that could be paid for by his housing allowance. His room was never a home – it was just a place to stash his body for the night. He couldn't be bothered to look for something better; one room is as good or bad as the next room when your mind is homeless.

His street – The Ridgeway – is one of those anonymous sub-urban streets that are made extraordinary by their hyper-ordinari-ness. People live here, but there are no signs of life. My friend Evie comes with me. Jack used to rent a room at Evie's place, until she had to ask him to leave. He wrecked his room and left owing her money, which was typical of The Other Jack.

We are met at Jack's place by the caretaker, a middle-aged man wearing a t-shirt, shorts and a solemn face that looks as if its been put on for this meeting, like a tie for a funeral. He has sad blue eyes. "I didn't really know Jack," he says, "but I wish I had". His voice is soft with a hint of self-blame as if he could have done something to save Jack. He tells us, "Jack was very unhappy."

The caretaker describes the house as a "friendly place" where the tenants would sometimes meet in the kitchen for dinner. "But not Jack. He kept to himself. He used to get a lot of takeaways. I found a big stack of old pizza boxes in his room," and then with a dramatic pause adds, "and a pool of blood."

He shakes his head. "It wasn't very nice."

His use of understatement here suggests that as a big player in this story of the strange young man who killed himself, he too has suffered. The caretaker then leads us up the stairs to Jack's room. "This is it. Room 4" and he unlocks the door and we troop in.

It's so small! A tiny, white cubicle of a room with a window that looks out on a back garden where nothing grows. I'd assumed that Jack's room would still look like Jack's room but clearly a new tenant has moved in and all traces of Jack – his messy life and bloody death have been scrubbed away. The normality of suburbia has been restored. I wonder if the new boy in Jack's room knows the story about the smell and the dead boy who slept in his bed?

"It was here," says the cleaner pointing to the floor just in front of the door, "that I found the blood. Right here. It wasn't very nice."

And I think: *Yeah, I got the pool of blood bit mate. Move on.*

I walk around trying to feel something; grief, anger, guilt anything but this emotional emptiness; but nothing can penetrate the blandness of this room and its oppressive ordinariness. I take out my phone and start filming like a tourist at a sight of historical interest. I reason that maybe, watching this later when I'm alone will evoke the right feelings. It's really the back of the door that I want to film. I keep trying to tempt out my grief by telling myself: this is it! Here's the exact spot where Jack died. The place of his execution. Look! See it! Touch it! Hear it! The past wants to speak…

And I think: shut the fuck-up!

It's just a door. And you can't expect doors, old photos, baby wrist bands, music and memories to make you feel the things you want to feel.

Sometimes the mundane refuses to release its magic and cast its spell and this is one of them.

I say to the cleaner, "Can we go get his stuff now? I need to get back." Cleaner and Evie look at each other, unsure if this is callousness or grief talking.

The cleaner then takes us out to the garden where Jack's things have been packed in dustbin bags and three blue IKEA bags. This is what Jack leaves behind:

1   Books that include *Romper Stomper, Trainspotting,* Stephen King's *It*.

2   DVDs: Mostly nasty horror films and gangster dramas.

3   Old clothes (jeans, hoodies) his trainers.

4   Posters: A4-sheets of death skeleton nu-metal posters he's printed off the internet.

5   Plastic bags full of various forms of medication.

6   Small bands for tying his hair back.

7   And strangely, packets of green scouring pads.

And that's Jack's stuff. The police have taken his laptop, iPod, passport (inside which they found a small seal wrap containing a white powdery substance) and a small glass crack pipe. But the autopsy found no evidence of drug usage.

Evie suggests we sort through the bags to donate to charity and the cleaner agrees but I want to get away. "Just dump it" I say, "Dump it all." I want out. I want to go home.

The cleaner must think what a cold and uncaring bastard that dad of Jack's is. When we get ready to go Evie and cleaner hug. Not a swift farewell hug but a big let-me-feel/share-your-grief hug.

Oh Christ, will I have to do a grief hug too? I hold out my hand for a shake, but no I'm pulled into the cleaner's hug.

One thing I've learned is that in the brotherhood of grief, all men and women must hug.

10

Old Me Vs New Me

2015

Now that I've buried Jack and collected his things, a chapter of my life is over and the question I face is: now what?

Should I get some help? Join a grief support group or go into therapy? What am I going to do with my life, just drift along churning out frothy features – or take this opportunity to change my life and help others in my position?

Why not? Other dads – and mothers – do it. They lose a child and find a whole new purpose to life by becoming suicide activists. A month before Jack died in June 2015, Anna Mansfield – a forty-four-year-old married mother of two small children – committed suicide. Anna's father, Michael Mansfield QC and his wife Yvette, set up a social support group called Silence of Suicide (SOS) that provides support for people who are thinking of suicide or have lost a loved one to suicide.

Also in 2015, eighteen-year-old Edward Mallen died of suicide and his father Steven Mallen joined the Zero Suicide Alliance. He has devoted his life to campaigning to prevent all suicides. And all over the UK grieving mums and dads and brothers and sisters are out there doing their bit to prevent more grieving mums and dads and brothers and sisters.

But I did nothing. Of course there were times when I wondered if this was the right thing to do? I would have this inner debate in my head between what I called the Old Me and the New Me. Old Me was resistant to change or doing anything other than letting time do its healing thing. New Me – that is the man I could become – wanted to turn this tragedy into something good by helping others.

Their arguments went something like this…

New Me: You must get some help! You can't just suffer in silence. Nothing will change unless you take charge of your life and try to change. Why don't you go to a group meeting of suicide survivors? Just give it a go.

Old Me: No way! For a start, I hate that term "suicide survivor". It makes it sound like I've done something worthy, I've overcome the odds and I have survived! No thanks Gloria Gaynor! I've done nothing. And secondly, I'm not going to sit in a room full of strangers sipping tea from a polystyrene cup and sharing my sad story and shedding tears with people who have come to share their sad stories and tears with strangers! No thanks!

New Me: You're a suicide snob! You look down on people who turn to other people for help and for comfort.

Old Me: Look, if that's what people want to do then fine. Go ahead, knock yourself out. Me, I'm not into all that sharing shit. See-Me-Feel-Me-Touch-Me-and-my-pain! Yuck!

New Me: Ok. What about going into therapy? You have a lot of unresolved issues with Jack to deal with and until you sort those out, you won't be able to grieve or get on with your life.

Old me: Fuck therapy! Spoilt white people of the Western world think everything can be solved by going into therapy. Everyone I know is in therapy – and none of them are getting any better. People have dealt with personal tragedy for thousands of years without therapy. They learn to cope with fortitude, endurance and inner strength.

New Me: Oh really? How's it going with the old fortitude, endurance and strength remedy? Is it really helping you?

Old Me: Ok. Fair point. Let's just say it's something I'm working on.

New Me: Think about it – all that soul-crushing suffering you're experiencing, and for what? Without doing good, without finding purpose and making something positive out of your loved one's death, all that's left behind is nothing but pain, guilt, doubt and distress. And that's it. That's your lot. No better you. No better tomorrow. No spiritual growth. From now on it's just you and your little sad life and the infinite ache of your loss. Is that all you want?

Old Me: No, it's not what I particularly want but that's the way it is. You can have your little grief goodies or you can face the truth.

New Me: If you're not going to help yourself then you should help others in your situation. If doing something can save one life, isn't it worth doing?

Old Me: What makes you think I could save anyone's life? I couldn't save my own son's life. Anyway, what's the point? You get one person to come down off the ledge – and another person takes their place. Suicide is a sad fact of existence.

New Me: So what do you plan to do with Jack's death – sit back and mope and sneer at the cake bakers and the marathon runners and the dads who in the name of their dead child want to do something good? Wouldn't you like to be one of those dads who make a difference?

Old Me: No. Yes. I guess so.

New Me: Listen to these words from a father whose son died of an illness: "I realised that my destiny was to live my life in a way that would make my son proud. The awareness that I could add goodness to my son's life by doing good in his name motivates me to this day." Wouldn't you like to do something like that, and make Jack proud?

Old Me: But Jack is dead! And he's not going to be proud of what I do or don't do. You can add goodness to the world in your son's name, but you can't add goodness to your son's life – especially when they're dead! Sorry. Only your son could do that. Look, I understand that these dads are determined to make something good out of something terrible. But that which is most terrible can not be tamed or accommodated by good and noble intentions and actions. It is a brutal, merciless, unforgiving and unchangeable thing. Death is indifferent to your tears, to the sound of your heart breaking and all your good deeds – and that is why it's so terrible!

New Me: I agree. You can't change the nature of terrible things – but you can change how you respond to them. What about Viktor Frankl, the Austrian psychologist and author of *Man's Search for Meaning*? In 1944 he was sent to Auschwitz where he endured five months of slave labour. His experiences in a Nazi concentration camp convinced him that no matter how terrible things are, we are always free to choose how we respond to them. "When we are no longer able to change a situation," wrote Frankl, "we are challenged to change ourselves." People can flourish, grow and become better and more fulfilled during the most terrible times of their lives.

Old Me: Please, spare me the old be-positive-embrace-your-grief-do-something-good lectures of yours! Don't go all Oprah on me!

New Me: Do you know who you remind me of?

Old Me: I dunno. Every self-pitying sad-sack of a dad in the world?

New Me: You remind me of Jack. You're so much like him. Remember how you used to say to him, why won't you ever try to overcome your unhappiness and give things a go? You used to complain about his "relentless negativity" and now look at you! You could use this terrible event to start afresh and become that man you always wanted to be: that better man.

Old me: Ok. I admit people can change and I should change.

I could cultivate patience and practice kindness with people.

I could become the Super Dad I always wanted to be with my son Dexter.

I could use my limited time on earth to do good.

I could be mindful of every precious moment of every precious day.

I could be happy to hug people.

I could drop my cynical, wise-cracking journalistic persona and no longer fear sincerity.

I could organise charity events to raise money for suicide prevention groups.

I could comfort other 'survivors of suicide' and say: I feel your pain without a trace of irony or embarrassment.

I could stop my silly dating column and write about the issue of mental health and fight the stigma associated with suicide.

I could even write a memoir about my son's suicide that critics will call 'brave' and 'moving'.

And there will come the day when I will be able to tell devastated parents that I managed to make something good come out of something bad – *and you can do it too*! And I will help you.

New Me: This is great news! Well done you!

Old Me: Thanks bro. But it's never going to happen because I hate all this positive grief shit.

New Me: what?

Old Me: Why must every tragedy have a happy ending and a positive outcome? I don't want to become a happy-shiny-grief-zombie doing good. If other dads want to, that's up to them.

They do it as a kind of personal therapy or a form of secular redemption – and there's nothing wrong with that. Ok, so I won't get an MBE for raising awareness of mental health issues, big deal.

New Me: So what are going to do instead?

Old Me: Here's my plan. One sunny morning I will crawl under my duvet and never come out.

Or, I will sit on the sofa and decompose in front of the television watching afternoon soaps, sipping gin, shrouded in swirls of cigarette smoke, staring into space and trying to drown out the tick-tock-tick-tock of my self-torment.

I will take every drug I can get my hands on.

I will become thin and gaunt and I will smell bad.

And inside my head, Jack will mock me for my pong and ask:

Dad, do you have to stink up the place?

I will call ex-girlfriends up at 3am in the morning and weep and complain that I'm so lonely that I want to die. And when they leap into a cab, travel across London, and ring my door bell I will shout over the intercom: *FUCK OFF! CAN'T YOU LEAVE ME ALONE!*

And I will feel a disgust for myself that is greater than my sorrow for my son. But of course this won't happen either. Why? Because I don't feel that kind of pain. And I hate myself for not feeling that kind of pain. The problem is I just don't hate myself *enough*. But hey, I'm working on it!

New Me: Ok, you know this is just your grief talking.

Old Me: No, it isn't. It's me. It's who I am and who I will always be.

New Me: Ok. What can I say? I only hope that one day you will change your mind.

• • •

2022

That was then and this is now: and I'm ready for that change. I realise that I have an obligation to try and help others in my situation. I have a duty of care – we all have that duty to various degrees – but I'm not sure what to do.

I could take part in one of those fund-raising activities for a suicide prevention/mental health charity – but I'm too much of a chicken to do the parachute jump; I'm too unfit to tackle the three peak mountain climb or run a marathon; I'm too impatient to sit through a gala evening dinner; I'm too stupid for a pub quiz and I'm too old to shave my head, wear a false nose for a week or see how many hot dogs I can eat in a minute. I guess I could make the "£8 donation that can save a life" to the charity Papyrus but that seems pretty meagre.

Suddenly Old Me pops-up with a suggestion: I know. Why don't you organize a support group for writers who have written a 'beautiful', 'brave' and 'moving' memoir of loss and can't find a publisher? These people are traumatized and they need your help! You could have a fundraising event where they go and read from their book and share hugs and tears with the public! You could raise a lot of money that way!

Me: Jack, why are you sniggering?

Jack: Because it's funny?

Me: Maybe I could just write this book about you and me? That will be my contribution to making a difference.

Jack: Dad, I hate to break it to you but nobody wants to read that sort of thing – especially from an old white guy. Sorry.

Me: Ok, what do I do?

Jack: I dunno. Maybe there's nothing you can do. You and all those people – the suicide prevention lot – look, they all mean well. But at the end of the day some of us will just want to die, and there's nothing you can do about that.

Me: I don't believe that. Or I should say, I don't want to believe that.

Jack: Yeah, nobody does. But that doesn't mean it's not true. You don't get it do you? People like you just can't imagine being in a place where to die is better than to live? Just to make it fucking stop: the fear, the terror, the loneliness, the self-hating, the total nothingness of your shit existence. The thing is dad, you never understood that I was dead even before I died.

Me: No I didn't, because I didn't believe it. I thought I could help you to live.

Jack: You tried your best and I don't think you or any parent is to blame – what you forget is that we can fuck-up our own lives without the help of mummy and daddy. I did – and kids, you can too!

11

Troubled Times

One day in July 2005 I get a message from Julie. "Jack had a breakdown! I've put him in the Priory. Bloody Nora, that place costs a bloody packet! Cheers!"

Jack was eighteen. He'd been living with his mum in Brighton when it happened. Brighton is a seaside town with a shabby charm. Along with its fading façade of old world gentility Brighton has a druggy-indie-alternative lifestyle scene that makes it the perfect playground and hiding place for boys like Jack; boys on the run from responsibility and adulthood.

Jack didn't have a job and not much interest or an incentive to find one. He lived with his mum for free and she provided financial support. As far as I can tell his days were spent on YouTube, Facebook, learning to play guitar, eating junk food, watching horror films and getting high on weed and magic mushrooms. He did sign up for a private music school, but quickly dropped out.

Whenever I asked him about his life in Brighton he always said he was looking for a job and looking for a band to join. He knew that's what I wanted to hear. So he went through the pantomime of having a plan and purpose.

It was all good, he said. All good. No need to worry dad.

And then the voices came…

Voices inside his head saying all kinds of scary stuff; he was damned and was going to hell and there he would rot and burn forever! At first he thought he was just going crazy – but then he became convinced that the voices were telling the truth; he *was* damned and he *was* going to hell!

For a while Jack tried to keep his voices to himself but the terror got too much and he broke down and told his mum that he was going to hell. No you're not! said his mum. You're going to the Priory. Come on. Off we go.

● ● ●

Jack's breakdown took me by surprise. Why had this happened? And where did all this crazy burn-in-hell stuff come from? I'm a non-practicing Jew and he'd never been subjected to any religious teachings from his mum or me.

Of course I knew that Jack had problems. He'd entered adolescence suffering from anxiety and the occasional bout of depression. He'd also had a period of bad acne and being overweight. But I wasn't that worried about him. After all, our divorce was behind him and Julie and I were getting on well. And Jack had done well enough in his A-levels that he got a place at Queen Mary's University to read English Literature. I told myself that Jack didn't really have serious mental health issues; he just had serious teenager issues like anxiety, sadness, bad skin and terrible taste in music. It would pass. So I would have said that on balance, Jack was pretty happy or at least content.

But Jack was living a secret life; hiding his secret self from his mum and me. I had no idea that at fourteen he was taking magic mushrooms and that by the time he was eighteen he was smoking skunk regularly. I later learned that he'd actually sat with me at the dinner table *stoned*. And I, Mr. Teenage Acid Head himself, had no idea he was flying high. I was one of those dads who knew all about drugs – having experienced them first hand – and yet I was no more aware of my son's stoned state of mind than your typical straight-laced dad who'd never smoked a joint in his life.

And I had no idea that Jack was self-harming; cutting his arms with razor blades. I'd always assumed that was something teenage girls did. Then one day I saw his arms and the hieroglyphics of self-hate – all those cuts, scars, slash marks – and I was shocked.

Life Lesson Number Five: *Don't Assume You Know Your Kids*

We think that because we live in an enlightened age where it's "good to talk" that we can be open and intimate with our children and thus creating a space in which they feel comfortable to tell us what's really on their mind and what they're really feeling.

Unlike earlier generations of distant dads, we modern dads like to think we have an emotional literacy that allows us to read the signs of unhappiness. But certain kids are very good at hiding their problems and their pain and you don't know that anything is seriously wrong until it's too late.

You read about these kids in the newspapers all the time. There's the 'happy' teenage boy with the 'bright future' and the popular 'bubbly girl' who was so much fun and loved by everyone.

They have loving parents and to the world they have no worries: and then one day they're found dead in their bedroom.

These suicide kids are masters of deception; con-artists of the highest calibre for they have managed to convince family and friends that they are normal, happy, functioning individuals. How do they do that? How do they never give their damaged selves away? How do they keep their secret longing to die secret? Not for them the eating disorders, the swinging moods, the scars of self-harming or the sounds of psychotic trash metal seeping out of their bedroom, that sets parental alarm bells ringing.

All their pain and torment is held in check by the straightjacket of a smile. They give nothing away. Even on the day they decide to die, right up to the moment that they go to their bedroom – they walk off to their own extermination as if they were just popping out to pick up something from the local newsagent and will be back in a sec. For the families they leave behind it's a double blow of shock: shocked by the way they died and shocked by the way they lived and lied.

• • •

I always thought that Jack and I were close, that he could always talk to me if there was something on his mind. But during the early period of his adolescence he never told me how he really felt. I suspect that's because he wanted to protect me from worry or hurt.

Instead he talked to his buddy Poria. When he was fifteen Jack told him he was "depressed" and when Poria asked what he meant by that, Jack said he felt down most of the time. And when Poria asked him why, Jack said there was no particular reason: "I just don't feel happy."

At sixteen Jack went off to sixth-form college to study for A-Levels in Film, History and English Literature. Jack described himself in those days as "a bit of a geek" and a "loser". But "fairly intelligent" and someone with strong opinions. According to his best schoolmate Jake, Jack had a "sick sense of humour" which Jake shared.

A child psychologist would have had a field day with a kid like Jack. They would see signs of trouble in his sick sense of humour and his love of horror films; especially nasty ones like *The Second House on The Left* and *Hellraiser*. As a young boy Jack had been fascinated by horror stories and pictures of movie monsters. He drew the kind of pictures that you always see in movies in the scene featuring the artwork of a 'disturbed' child (usually the opening credits to the sound of the soft tinkling piano). Pictures in colourful crayon that have that disturbing mix of sunny innocence and dark gore. Pictures where family and friends are being chased or sliced and diced up by satanic clowns or laughing zombies. Where the family cat is swinging from a tree and a school teacher has lost her head.

From an early age – around ten – Jack had been fascinated by a particular horror film character known as Pinhead from Clive Barker's film *Hellraiser*. Jack had not seen the film – I refused to let him because he was too young – but he had seen pictures of Pinhead in a horror magazine he used to read called *Fangoria*. Pinhead was an iconic figure for horror fans. He was a pin-up of pure pain; a white, hairless, demonic creature with a head made up of deep grids from which large nails stuck out. Jack used to ask me questions about Pinhead's condition and Pinhead's life as though he was a friend of the family or an eccentric uncle with a curious illness.

At the time I didn't think this fascination with horror was strange or revealed something significant about Jack's state of mind. But recently I read Brett Easton Ellis on his fascination as a young boy with horror films. For Ellis the horror films of the 1970s weren't just escapist entertainment for teenage thrill-seekers but true reflections of the reality of "adulthood and life itself…the disappointments I already witnessed in my parent's failing marriage."

Am I reading too much into Jack's boyhood taste for horror? What was he meant to draw – smiley suns, rainbows and pink prancing unicorns? What films should he have loved, to show that he was well-adjusted – animation films featuring cute animals and kooky insects? I don't know.

But instead of growing out of his fascination with horror – as teenage boys usually do – Jack grew into it. The bands he loved as a teenager – Insane Clown Posse, Slipknot, Murder Dolls, Marilyn Manson – took their look and sound from horror films. The picture he used for his Facebook page profile was of a corpse's head. The horror aesthetic was a key means for Jack to define who he was, what he liked and how he saw the world. Why did horror films strike such a chord in Jack? Why did the horror aesthetic become the prism through which he viewed life? I guess they reflected the way he saw and felt about the world.

Of course we can read too much into the obsessions of our children – but we can also read too little. Oh well, we tell ourselves, it's just a phase they're going through. I did the same when I was young. And then in retrospect, after something terrible has happened to them, the harmless fad looks like an alarm call that you failed to answer.

I plead not guilty to negligence. I can honestly say that I didn't know how bad things were for Jack – at least in those early teen years. But it was all there in front of me, right in my face and in my ears. That trash-metal music of his, screaming with pain and anger and self-disgust. Those films are full of horror, blood, fear and death. Put them together and what do they say? "It's all good."

• • •

I never thought that one day I'd be going to the Priory to visit a son of mine. It was a famous rehab place for drug-damaged rock stars and celebrities – not ordinary kids like Jack. When I went to visit him I was surprised by how happy he seemed. It was more like his club than a clinic and he was making new friends.

He showed me around the place and pointed out the people he knew. There was the "sweet American Christian girl" with bandages on her wrists who kept trying to kill herself and the quiet teenage boy who took a heroin overdose and said he would do it again as soon as possible. "The people here are seriously fucked-up!" said Jack in a way that suggested that by comparison, his problems weren't so bad. Clearly, Jack found it comforting to be in a community of damaged people; they put his own problems in perspective.

After a few weeks Jack left the Priory. He was diagnosed as depressed and at risk of self-harm, but he was given anti-depressants and became an outpatient who returned weekly for therapy and I went with him. Both Julie and I were relieved that he was under proper medical supervision. And Jack told me he found his therapist very helpful and his medication (Quetiapine and Escitalopram) made him feel a lot better. The voices were gone and the anxiety attacks were less frequent. Jack was feeling good about his life. It looked like he had a fresh start.

And then I went and fucked-it up.

On leaving the Priory Jack asked if he could come and stay with me for a bit.

"Of course you can," I said.

And then I asked: "What do you mean by a bit?"

"I don't know. Six months or so?"

"Six months!? Jack…look…that might be a problem."

"What? I can't live in my own home anymore?"

He sounded confused. Hurt.

"No!" I said, "Of course you can stay…let's just see how things go."

I wanted to do everything a Good Dad could do to help his troubled son. I wanted to be a part of his life. I wanted to be there for him. I wanted to give him the love and security he needed.

I just didn't want to have him living with me; which was the one thing he wanted and needed.

But by then I had a new wife (Maxine) and baby son and that meant I had a new life. And I was so happy with my new family and I loved my new life. Maxine had organized the total renovation and decoration of the flat. It was like living in a new flat without having to move. New flat, new wife, new child; I had been granted what every middle-aged man dreams of: a fresh start.

And up pops an old problem called Jack.

He wanted a place in my new life. He wanted to move back into the home he had grown up in. He wanted his old room back; the one with the *Aladdin* wallpaper and the *Sonic the Hedgehog* duvet. But a new boy was sleeping in his room.

I don't know what Jack thought about my new family. When Maxine and I had got married in 2004 he had not come to the wedding. I'm not sure why. (We'd probably had a row.) As for his new half-brother he took a polite interest in him but nothing more. (His mum also had a new man in her life who she eventually married.) I know little about Jack's relationships with girls his own age at this time, but I get the impression that nothing serious had really happened.

When I first raised the prospect of Jack moving in with us for "a bit" I could tell Maxine was worried.

"How long is a bit?" she asked.

"Just till he gets himself sorted," I said.

Oops. Wrong answer. The Jack sorting process could take decades.

"Well, you have to do what you need to do to help your son," she said.

It was a generous response but I wondered if the protective lioness mum in her thought: *I don't want that fucking nutcase with the drugs and crazy voices in his head around my baby! Tell him to fuck-off and go live with his mum!*

Did I secretly share that fear too? No. I knew Jack was no danger to Dexter or anyone else – except me. He was a clear and present danger to my newfound happiness. I knew from experience that living with Jack was difficult – for both of us. I feared we'd be rowing. That the whole atmosphere in the flat would go from calm to crazy within days of his arrival.

And it did.

We started having terrible rows about domestic things like his reluctance to help around the flat. We rowed about his messiness. We rowed about his moodiness. We rowed about what he was doing with his life. We rowed about what he wasn't doing with his life. At times these were furious and ugly rows. To my utter shame I once threw a small dustbin he had not emptied out at him.

And yet at the time I felt that I was the one who was suffering an injustice. My reasoning went like this: I give you so much support and I ask so little of you in return…just once a week take out the rubbish. And you never do because of some lame excuse. It will take you less than five minutes – and you can't even do that! What a shitty son you are!

Of course, this wasn't about taking out the rubbish; it was about taking responsibility. I was doing my Dad thing. I wanted Jack to be the kind of person who could take care of things that had to be done for himself or for other people. But he didn't want to take out the rubbish because he couldn't be "arsed". It could be done, thought Jack, at some other time that suited him and not the designated night for rubbish collection the following morning. The way he saw it was: who cares if the rubbish is taken out on Wednesday or a Friday? It's just rubbish! It will get collected. What's dad getting so worked up about?

I'm fully aware of the irony of the situation. I wanted Jack to grow up and be responsible and when he failed to do that I retaliated with a childlike temper tantrum. In retrospect, I realise that the bin incident first revealed to me just how angry I was at Jack. And it wouldn't be long before I discovered how angry Jack was with me.

Don't worry, I'm not going to give you the Life Lesson about not rowing with your teenage children because that's impossible to do. You will row. You will rage. And if your child dies you will be filled with regret. If your child lives, you'll laugh at those rows or you won't remember them.

Eventually the rowing got too much and I suggested Jack move out and stay with my parents in their big house in Islington. I explained to Jack that when I was around his age I was always fighting with my dad and so I moved out and went and stayed with another family in Kentish Town and I loved it. And he would too.

It seemed the perfect solution. My parents – Jay and Fran – were old bohemians, who lived in a big run-down house and regarded any kind of domestic cleaning as a bourgeois neurosis. Stepping into their house was going back to the late 1960s; it was funky and filthy and Jack would fit in perfectly.

I said, "If you were with your grandparents you wouldn't have me moaning at you all the time. It would ease things between us."

Jack was silent.

Look, I said. Why not try it? If you're unhappy you can move back in here?

With reluctance Jack agreed to give it a go. But I knew – and he knew – that once he was out he would never come back.

• • •

It felt liberating to have Jack out of the flat. I could breathe. He tended to radiate gloom the way other people exude body odour.

I honestly believed that living with my parents was a good idea. It was a short bus ride away and Jack would always be welcome to come back to his old home and have dinner and hang out. And whenever he came to dinner – and he came about once a fortnight – I checked on his life with my parents and from what he told me, it seemed that Jack liked living there. He never once said or hinted that he'd like to move back to his old home with me. But that was just the silence of his pride.

It was only after his death did I learn from Poria and Jake that Jack had been "devastated' when, as Poria put it to me "you kicked him out of his home." Jack's good friend Jake said the same thing, "he was devastated."

And now I can see what I did to him and how he must have felt...

This was my home and now you're kicking me out, just because you have a new family? Fuck that! What about your old family? What about me? Don't I matter? I'm in trouble. I need help. I need a home. I need a dad. I need you. And you're kicking me out! You're always doing this "I want to be a good dad" stuff – is this what a good dad would do? Thanks dad.

Jack was that it? Did it feel like that?

Spot on dad! You really fucked me over on that one. But hey, don't beat yourself up about it. Shit happens.

12

Down The toilet

At the age of twenty-four Jack was drifting in and out of a series of low-paid jobs with no future and drifting in and out of rock bands with no chance. Two years after I'd kicked him out he was still living with my parents in their toilet on the landing. It's a small, rundown cubicle with bare brick walls. There's decaying linoleum on the floor and the loo seat resembles a coated tongue. It's usually cold and grimy and Jack could not fully stretch from one end of the cubicle to the other. Inside he had his sleeping bag, a black dustbin bag full of clothes and his laptop. I should point out that it was a toilet still used by family and guests.

Jack could have stayed in a proper room that was near my father's room in the basement. It was small and cluttered with family junk, but it looked out onto a beautiful wild garden and with a bit of effort he could have made it into a really nice room of his own. When I suggested this to him Jack just said what he always said: "Nah. I can't be arsed." He claimed that he preferred the toilet on the landing.

I struggled to understand this: my son is twenty-four-years-old and living in a toilet! And the most shocking thing is that my son is actually *happy* living in the toilet. When Jack first told me he was happy living in the toilet I was horrified.

"Please tell me you're joking," I said.

"No. Honest. I like it. It's cosy."

"It's a fucking toilet for God's sakes!" I cried. "You're living in a toilet!"

"So?"

Jack felt no embarrassment or shame about living in a toilet. He told me he'd brought a girl back there to spend the night in the toilet with him – but the two of them couldn't fit inside, so she had to go home.

I said with heavy-handed sarcasm, "Boy, I bet she was devastated at not spending a night of hot romantic passion on a toilet floor!"

Jack didn't pick up on my sarcasm and said, "Yeah, she was. I was upset too."

Living In A Toilet: A Philosophical Inquiry

What is a parent to do when they discover their son is living in a toilet – and is *happy* living in a toilet? Should I, like a good bourgeois parent, be horrified at the poverty of my son's aspirations and give him another lecture on the need to get his act together and get on in life?

Or do I take the position my dear old bohemian dad took? I once went to see him in his basement lair during lunchtime to discuss the Jack toilet issue. I found him behind his desk wearing his fedora hat and a seersucker suit. He had a joint dangling from the corner of his mouth and he was sipping a martini, listening to jazz and working on his memoirs. "Hey kiddo, what's up?" he said.

When I told him my worries about Jack living in the toilet he looked at me with a scrunched-up face of disapproval and said: "Don't be so bourgeois! Let the kid do his own thing. If he's happy living in a toilet – that's fine. If not, he'll figure something out. He's a smart kid."

"Oh yeah?" I say, "If he's so smart how come he's living in your toilet?"

"Let's just say he's got good taste in décor!"

• • •

Don't get me wrong. I'm all for people doing their own thing – at least in theory. But when your child's "thing" is a living-in-a-toilet thing, it's different. I could picture Jack as an old man, with no wife, no family, no income living on his own in that same toilet. And when social services come to take him away and put him into care he will say: *but I was happy there! It was cosy!*

Downward mobility is the great middle-class nightmare. But I was – supposedly – a good bohemian who looked down on that middle-class obsession with working hard, getting on in life and becoming successful. And Jack, true to his bohemian heritage, had stepped off the conventional conveyor belt of middle-class life – university/work/marriage/mortgage/family – only to end up in his grandparent's toilet.

Part of me was happy to have a free-thinking, unconventional bohemian son – but did he have to be *that* bloody bohemian? I was worried that Jack – unlike the children of my friends who were in their mid-twenties – didn't seem to have any aspirations or ambitions of any kind. Yes, he played bass guitar in various bands, but had no desire for success or longing to write songs. It was as if he'd given up on life, even before he had begun to live it.

I once asked him: "don't you want to do something with your life"?

Naah, said Jack. He told me he just wanted to get a 'crappy job' that paid him enough money so he could rent a room that wasn't too shitty, hang out with friends, listen to music, get stoned and party. In other words, he wanted a life of perpetual adolescence; one free from the drudgery and responsibilities of adulthood. But also one, I suspect, free of the anxiety of having to go out into the world and compete for success and risk failure.

But Jack didn't see it that way. He thought he was rejecting the values of conventional society. He told me he wasn't into all that "success stuff…You know, like having a career…making loads of money…buying a house…having kids…being a happy-smiley consumer. No thanks! Not my thing."

But unlike those other groups and sub-cultures that flourished in the 20th century – from Bloomsbury to the Beats – Jack didn't see himself as a rebel or a champion of an alternative culture or way of life. Damaged and disaffected young men like Jack had no revolutionary texts, no interest in anarchism or Marxism because they had no belief in the possibility of anything ever getting better for individuals or society as whole. Their world view was a form of nihilism – I called it shitism – based on three basic ideas:

1   I am shit.

2   People are shit.

3   Life is shit.

From this it followed that Jack saw his only option was to get stoned as much as possible.

And then die.

I Do A Jack

In 2010 I had the following conversation with Jack that went something like this.

Me: You're a very intelligent and capable boy.

Jack: Cheers.

Me: But I worry about you. You're twenty-four and you're living in your grandparents' toilet! This is no life.

At this Jack gave me a big grin and said, Dad, you're fifty-four and living in your parents' storage room in the basement. This is no life.

He was right. In 2010 Maxine and I split up and I moved back in with my parents for just a bit until I could get myself sorted – or so I told myself. So here I was back living with Jack under one roof. We were both exiles from family life, a bit lost and looking for shelter. My parents had provided me with the reassuring place of my childhood – now that I was living there I realised that's exactly what Jack had wanted from me but I'd said no.

• • •

Life Lesson Number Six: *Don't Compare Your Kids With Other Kids*

I tried not to compare Jack with other kids, especially those of my friends. But of course I did. (We all do.) We know it's a ridiculous and unnecessary practice that reveals our hidden status anxiety and social aspirations, and yet we can't help doing it.

When Jack was in his mid-teens I would tell myself that he had his own Jack thing and that was good enough. But then I would hear a friend talk about what their son or daughter had just accomplished and I'd immediately think: why can't Jack do that? Why can't he be like other kids and do things and achieve things?

I had a good friend whose son was a similar age to Jack. My friend was proud of his son and rightly so; he was always winning prizes and coming top of the class. Even though he was good at school Jack never won anything, but then neither did I. My friend's son was brilliant at sports, painting and languages. After telling me about the triumphs of his son, my friend would do the polite thing and ask, "How's Jack doing?" and there would be this awkward pause and I'd say what I always said, "Oh, he's doing good. You know…" and I'd quickly change the conversation.

That Jack never won anything or distinguished himself in any way, wasn't easy to accept. But I told myself it was more important to be a good person than to acquire glittering-prizes – fully aware that's exactly what we parents of under-achieving children always tell ourselves as a form of compensation.

One day my friend had some good news he wanted to share with me; his son had got into Oxford. He glowed with parental pride. I was just about to go into my usual, "well-done-that's-great-news!" routine when I felt something snap inside.

The years of congratulating him – and other parents – on the triumphs of their children took its toll. I knew what was coming and I said to myself: *Please don't do it! Don't go there. Stay silent. Just smile. Congratulate him on his son getting into Oxford. This is not a My-kid-vs-Your-Kid competition. Remember: the success of his son in no way reflects on your son and on you. Got it? Good. Now shut up.*

And out it popped: "Oxford? Big-fucking-deal! Jack has got into rehab! The Priory no less. Beat that, bitch!"

My friend laughed. Nervously.

And so did I.

• • •

Why did I say that?

I was partly satirising the one-upmanship of middle-class parents; or so I told myself. And even though I'd always claimed to loathe the look-at-my-brilliant-child competitiveness that middle-class parents go in for, I also felt a pang of parental envy. Like the good, inverted bohemian snob that I was, I looked down on those parents whose boasts about their brilliant little darlings – which were really boasts about themselves – bored everyone at dinner parties. But the truth was: I wanted to boast about my son too.

I wanted for once – just once! – to be proud of him and tell family and friends all about something Jack had accomplished. It didn't have to be a place at Oxford or him landing some prestigious, high-paid job in a law firm or the City. Just to be able to say: Guess what? Jack's band got signed to a record company! Or, Jack has written this amazing novel! Or Jack did this…Jack did that…Jack just did…*something*.

I just wanted that Proud Parent Moment.

And what's that exactly? I don't really know but I imagine you just feel a swelling in your heart and maybe you get moist around the eyes because your kid has done this amazing thing. (Actually, it doesn't have to be that amazing.) And it doesn't have to come from what your child does; it can happen just by the way they look. Imagine a father seeing his daughter, his little girl on her wedding day all dressed up and grown-up and beaming with happiness; don't tell me that man doesn't have a Proud Parent Moment.

Or you can have it when a dad sees his son in his first suit. That first suit is a significant moment in a boy's journey to being a man. I got my first suit at fifteen and in my twenties I would borrow my dad's suits; he was a stylish man and had a great collection of them. But Jack hated suits. I never once saw him in a stylish suit and thought: *my, what a handsome young man you've become!*

The only time Jack would put on a suit – one of my old ones – was when he went off for a job interview. I'd always looked forward to seeing Jack in a suit – with a shirt and tie – imagining that some sort of fairy tale transformation would take place and he'd no longer be the fucked-up kid with the dreads and a head full of darkness, but a stylish, confident, go-getting young man with a bright future.

Old or new, cheap or expensive, suits always looked bad on Jack. It was as if coming into close physical contact with him, the suit would wilt and die. And not because of size or style either, but because Jack just wasn't a suit kind of guy. To Jack suits were for Suits. Still, he had to put one on to find a job, but he resented this unnecessary and ridiculous charade demanded by the "dickheads" of the world. And always, his attempt to look respectable was so botched that it was kind of touching in its patheticness. Jack would put on a suit, shirt and tie – and tie his hair back – and take off for a job interview looking like a petty criminal dressed for his appearance in court.

Was it so terrible of me to want that moment of parental pride too? If only I could have given him a big hug and said, "Well done Jack, I'm so proud of you!"

Actually, I did once say that to him when Jack managed to get into Queen Mary's University to study English Literature.

"Yeah. Cheers," said Jack.

And then he popped my little bubble of parental pride when he added, "I'm only going to uni because I can't think of what else to do. I'm not really into in all that Eng-Lit shit. Man, it's so fucking boring!"

• • •

Did Jack ever want to make his parents proud? I think so.

I remember the saddest thing he ever said to me. It was in 2015 when he'd embarked on his new and short lived career as a drug dealer. He told me he was going to make a "shit load of money" and pay us, his parents, back. And then he said, "I'm going to make you and Julie so proud of me."

He'd never said anything like that before. Of course I thought about saying, "but we are proud of you Jack." But we both knew that would be a lie, so I said nothing. I should have lied. Boys like Jack sometimes need to hear lies; lies can ease the pain of living and give them a little hope. I've told a millions white lies in my lifetime so why couldn't I have told just that one little lie that might have done some good?

But what did Jack imagine would happen once his career as a drug dealer took off and the money started to roll in? That his mother and I, beaming with parental pride, would boast to friends, "Yes, our Jack is doing rather well in the drug trade. He's been promoted from handling small bags of weed in Camden Town to being in charge of the distribution of crack in the entire North London area!"

The Lost Boys

By the age of twenty-two Jack was one of the Lost Boys of life. They're the ones for whom the journey through adolescence and into adulthood never quite happens; they get stuck in the middle. No longer a kid, they're not quite an adult. Lost Boys become disconnected from life, living off-grid with no thought of the future. Theirs is the eternal now of those who have nowhere to go.

And their parents think: "What a shame. He was always such a bright and talented boy."

When it comes to taking care of the everyday business of life, Lost Boys are dysfunctional; they're big kids who can't cope with the demands of filling out forms, waiting in queues, turning up on time for important meetings.

In their early teens Lost Boys try and forge an identity out of tattoos and piercings, wild hair, rebel clothing and T-shirts with slogans that announce their inner afflictions and agonies: *Damaged Goods. Rage. Screwed. Fucked but Free*. They never grow out of this phase; they grow into it.

Lost Boys turn to drink and drugs to ease the pain of their problems; until the drink and drugs become the problem. Their good, liberal-minded parents understand and even tolerate their use of recreational drugs. After all, they too were once young and got high. They tell themselves it's just a phase; one he will grow out of.

But no, like Jack they grow into it – grow into the doper's way of life. From weed they move on to other drugs: acid, MDMA, coke, crack, speed and then comes the first line of heroin, but not their last. Their sweet boy has become a stoner – someone who is addicted to getting high as opposed to just one drug like heroin – and everyone knows what has happened but his parents.

The Ballad Of The Lost Boys

They go on medication, they come off medication.

They go into rehab, they come out of rehab.

They go into therapy, they come out of therapy.

They quit taking dope, they start taking dope.

They plan to do this, and they never do that.

For their mums and dads, first comes disappointment and then with the passage of time that disappointment ripens into despair. They want to do something to help their Lost Boy and yet they have grown to accept that there's nothing they can do to help him.

Lost Boys talk a lot about forming a band or making a film or some such creative endeavour. They have the dream, but not the discipline. They're too addicted to fun and too fidgety to sit down and do the creative graft necessary to make art. They are always starting projects they will never finish, and in time this will make them feel like a failure.

Lost Boys like Jack will tell you they don't give a fuck about any-thing: but that's just the hurt and pain talking tough. They're always surrounded by people, dashing from party to club to this girl, to the next. Getting wasted, getting wrecked, walking wounded.

They will talk about retraining for a new career, getting work experience, helping troubled kids or the homeless. And you're excited because this could be the turnaround you've been waiting for. And you do everything you can to help – until the day comes when you know it will never happen. It's just Lost Boy talk; dream babble fuelled by dope and desperation.

The Lost Boys drift through various low-paid jobs and blow various opportunities for high-paid ones that their parents provided. Instead of a career in law or the media, these young men become Artful Dodgers, urban scavengers who having been booted from the family home – usually for drugs, stealing or bad behaviour – live on their wits and welfare payments.

They surf the sofas of friends, find shelter in squats or shack-up with a girl who will love and take care of them until they can't take their madness and lies and drug use anymore, and ask them to leave.

They go on medication, they come off medication.

They go into rehab, they come out of rehab.

They go into therapy, they come out of therapy.

They quit taking dope, they start taking dope.

They plan to do this, and they never do that.

These Lost Boys can be very sweet. Charming. Kind. Considerate. And they can be complete psychos or major arseholes. They will steal your money, invade your privacy and break your heart. One minute you want to hold them in your arms – the next you want to strangle them.

Inevitably, there comes the day when the parents get a call from the police – and off you go to the local police station to bail out your Lost Boy.

You keep hoping that one day things will change; and one day you give up on that hope. All their fresh starts and new beginnings have been betrayed. The hardest thing to accept is that there comes a point when you have to accept the one thing you can never accept: there's nothing more you can do. You can't fix your damaged, darling Lost Boy.

But you wonder if this is just defeatism? Once you accept that there's nothing you can do, then you're accepting that your loved one is doomed to a life of depression – or maybe death.

I realise that these sad, damaged young men are not an easy group to sympathise with. They are often privileged middle or upper-class kids who had every opportunity to make something of their lives – and they took every opportunity to fuck-up every opportunity. But every sad and damaged young man began life as a sweet boy, who saw cars and got excited and shouted in amazement at the animals in the zoo.

What happens to these sad, young, damaged boys?

They go on medication, they come off medication.

They go into rehab, they come out of rehab.

They go into therapy, they come out of therapy.

They quit taking dope, they start taking dope.

They plan to do this, and they never do that.

And then one day the Lost Boy lets go of life.

And then. One. Two. Three. Boom.

They're dead.

13

Jack's Brain

One afternoon in 2012 Jack came over to my place in a distressed state. He tells me he's busted-up with his Polish girlfriend Melissa and he's attempted suicide. He wants me to make a will to leave Melissa what's left in his bank account, and he wants to buy a gun to shoot himself and he can't stop drooling, and he can't stop the nausea and by the way, "my brain is broken. I've got brain damage."

For the next three years Jack will remain utterly convinced that he has what he calls a "broken brain". He's even made up his own broken brain song that goes like this:

My brain, my brain. Who can help mend my broken brain?

My brain, my brain – who can tell me what happened to my brain?

Whenever he sings his brain song I give him a small, awkward pat on the back and a little pep talk that goes like this: No, your brain is not broken. You're just very depressed and going through a difficult time. Things can change. You can change. I can help you change. You'll see.

But Jack knows better. No, he says. His brain is broken and it can't be fixed. I'm fucked, he says. Totally fucked. When you have brain damage, Jack explains, there's no going back. You're not just fucked, you're fucked forever. And when you're fucked forever there's only one solution: suicide.

Nobody believes that Jack's brain is broken except Jack. You might think that Jack's brain damage diagnosis could be easily disproved; just get the kid a brain scan and it would show him that there was nothing wrong with his brain. He'd be relieved. He'd be happy. He could get his life back on track.

Jack had three different brain scans over a period of two years and none of them showed any damage and none of them did any good because Jack refused to accept the results of his scans. Like those religious fundamentalists who predict the exact day the world will end – and wake up the next morning, Jack always had an explanation for what the scan didn't show.

Dad, you don't understand. Some damage to the brain does not appear on brain scans.

Excuse me Dr Kildare, but when did you become a brain expert? How do you know you're right?

Man, just go online and take a look.

Nobody – none of the doctors, psychologists or mental health workers who saw Jack – believed that his brain was broken. Dr Ahmed, his GP, believes that Jack's brain belief is "a symptom of anxiety and depression." And the psychiatrist who examines Jack thinks "it's unlikely that he has a neurological condition. His belief that something serious has happened to his brain is probably a way of coping and making sense of why he is experiencing distressing symptoms."

But Jack knows they're wrong and he's right. His broken brain diagnosis is based on his extensive internet research. Jack's a Googletician, forever going online, visiting chat rooms, forums and watching YouTube videos for evidence that confirms his diagnosis.

Online Jack finds people who have suffered brain damage from car accidents or blows to the head, and they talk about the loss of their former self and how isolated and emotionally detached they have become from loved ones and the world at large. And Jack says: "That's me! That's exactly what I'm experiencing."

Jack finds an online chat forum for these people and spends a lot of time with his new brain-damaged friends. They bring him comfort. He feels less lonely but more miserable because he can't, because of his broken brain, think of anything to say to them.

This is a key turning point in Jack's story. With this diagnosis – I should say misdiagnosis – Jack has effectively sentenced himself to death. For once he becomes convinced that his brain is broken – that is, damaged beyond repair – he has lost forever the possibility that he could change, that life could change and he could be happy. This is the incineration of hope and in time this will lead to his death.

Jack claims it's because of his broken brain that he broke-up with Melissa and that he tried to kill himself by taking an overdose of heroin. Soon his broken brain becomes a catch-all explanation for everything big and small. It's why he can't get a job, go on the dole, make music, see people, post a letter, go to the shops, go for a walk with me, fill out a form or just get on a bus. But the damage of his broken brain goes deeper than an inability to function practically in the world.

Jack tells me he's no longer capable of feeling love and affection, of experiencing pleasure, of thinking or communicating with other people. The old me is dead, declares Jack.

I am an empty shell…I am a lump of nothing.

• • •

I tried to understand Jack's condition. We talked about it a lot and I made sympathetic noises. But I could never really grasp what he was going through. Over time I found it irritating when he went on and on about his broken brain and said things like: "people mean nothing to me" and "I have no feelings for anyone".

I took these comments personally and in the wrong way. I now see they were a plea for help, a way for Jack to explain his distressful disconnection from the world. But I felt hurt every time he said, "people mean nothing to me."

And I'd think: Ok. Fine. Then fuck-off. Go live somewhere else.

On one occasion talk of his condition triggered one almighty row between us.

"You stupid-fucking-drama-queen! How can you say that?! I don't believe that I could have a son who thinks that way. You're a moral moron!"

That's me yelling at Jack. I'm stomping around the living room, rolling my eyes and shaking my head in disbelief that my son could actually claim that as a result of his alleged "brain damage", he suffers *more* than *anyone* in the whole world. *Anyone! Anywhere!*

This is not some rhetorical flourish or an accidental exaggeration said in the heat of the moment; no, this is what Jack believes. What triggered this outburst of anger was when Jack said, "I look at the severely disabled or people who are dying of AIDS or cancer and I wish I had what they had. What I'm going through is so much worse."

See what I mean?

Eventually, I calm down and try to talk to him. I want to understand how he could think like this.

Me: Let me get this right. You're saying you suffer more than a child with cancer or some African child who is starving to death?

Jack: Yes!

Me: You suffer more than someone experiencing from physical torture?

Jack: Yes!

Me: A victim of rape?

Jack: Yeah. Definitely!

Me: Jack…how can you say that?

Jack: Because it's fucking true! At least those people can know love, they can relate and communicate with other people. They are still themselves, no matter what they've suffered. They are not alone. They are not dead inside.

Me: Oh Jack! For fuck's sake! Listen to yourself!

I must confess that I took some comfort from reading his mum's comment in her *Sunday Times* article about this tendency of Jack's. She wrote, "try putting up with that level of self-pity without losing your temper – and then you will be a saint."

I feel anger on behalf of those poor people he's mentioned; people who have *really* suffered. His words are so insensitive and so self-indulgent I want to scream! (Actually, I've already screamed.) The fact that he could not grasp the self-evident stupidity of his comments made it even worse.

So what am I to do? I could say that you're a middle-class, white man with parents who love you and doctors who care for you and though your life is painful, believe me, it's not the worst thing that could happen to a person because you can and you will come through this – you spoiled, indulged, ungrateful little shit!

Or I could act like a grown-up and try a little logic. Maybe something like: Ok Jack if your brain is really broken, how can you trust that it's telling you the truth about itself?

But no, I have to freak out and yell at him which is exactly what he doesn't need and what I don't want to do – and yet I do it. This is not the man and the dad I want to be – and yet this is the man and dad that I am. My intentions are so good; my behaviour is so bad. How are we to explain the vast chasm between who we aspire to be and the reality of how we act?

That is the subject of a whole other book. Let me just say if only I had spent more time on addressing my own problems and my own craziness, instead of focusing exclusively on Jack, I'd have had a better chance to be that man and that dad I wanted to be and Jack needed me to be.

At the time I failed to see that the truth or falseness of Jack's I-suffer-more-than-anyone claim was beside the point: it was true for him. This was his experience of his life. It felt like that. So instead of trying to understand why he thought this way, I just dismissed him as a self-indulgent drama queen.

The embarrassing truth is that I was the drama queen – making this huge angry drama out of a dumb remark by my very disturbed son. I was expecting Jack to think in a rational and reasonable way, to have that basic intuitive moral sense that out there in the world are people suffering far more than ourselves. In short: I was expecting Jack not to be Jack.

● ● ●

His brain, his brain…what happened to Jack's brain?

I think I know the answer: drugs happened.

He'd been taking drugs since he was fourteen. First mushrooms, then a bit of weed…then lots of weed. In 2007 he goes clubbing and starts taking ecstasy. The first five or six times it's fun; he experiences instant euphoria with no side effects. Jack has found, he thinks, the perfect drug.

But then one night he takes it and the next day he discovers something is wrong. "I had a thick layer of grain over my vision and a sense of unreality…it felt like the very core of my reality had been heavily muted, almost as if my soul had been ripped from my body…"

Jack is scared that he's done some real serious damage to himself so stops taking drugs. He goes back to Brighton to live with his mum. He goes back on his medication and he gets a job as a charity-fundraiser, he starts playing in a band and he's seeing friends. That post-ecstasy feeling of emptiness slowly resides. Feelings return. He can communicate with the outside world again. He's relieved that he's got his life back and his brain back working. Phew, that was a close one!

And then he does it all again. In 2010 he starts smoking a little weed…it's just a little weed. He's out with friends, he's had a few drinks, he's having fun and along comes a joint and…hey, why not? Where's the harm? So he has a little bit of weed but a little bit of weed inevitably becomes a lot of weed. Fuck it. Once you've crossed the line you might as well take whatever is around. Jack is taking any drug he can get his hands, nose and mouth on: coke, ketamine, LSD, heroin and even MDMA which is a powdered form of ecstasy – the very drug that zapped his brain in 2007. Jack's drug consumption is soon out of control. One day he takes three tabs of acid and smokes one of those legal highs – that are notoriously toxic – all at once. Jack is playing Russian roulette with his brain.

And then one night in 2012 Jack takes ecstasy again – and the internal fuse box of his brain, the one that keeps feelings and thoughts functioning suddenly fuses – and out go the lights. The next morning he is left with a feeling of emptiness, similar to the one he experienced back in 2007 after having taken the drug. Only this time the impact is deeper and more intense. He can't think coherently or articulate his thoughts. Around friends he can't speak and around his family he can't feel anything – or so he says.

Jack described his condition like this: "It's literally like being adrift in space; nothing feels real, nothing has any meaning; it's like a living death, or being buried alive…or frozen in a block of ice. I see this world and the people that I'm living in it with, but they are forever beyond my reach. I guess another fitting analogy would be the feeling of being underwater and looking up to the surface where you can see the people that love you trying to reach in to pull you out of the water but no matter how persistently they try you are totally beyond their reach as you continue to plummet to the bottom of the ocean."

What Jack is describing is a condition known as Dissociation, sometimes referred to as Derealisation. The term is used in different ways, but it usually describes an experience when you feel disconnected from the world or from yourself.

Here's how a young man called James described his experience of Dissociation and the similarity with Jack's experience is striking. "I felt emotionally numb. Any emotions I did feel just disappeared in an instant. I struggled to receive and give empathy. I didn't react much to anything happening around me. I had numbed senses, everything was lost, and nothing felt familiar. I couldn't remember my past; I had no self-identity and felt no connection to anybody or anything that surrounded me."

Like Jack, James suffered from an inability to communicate with people. James writes: "A source of anxiety was my inability to talk to others. I would always be in silence around people or complain about having no thoughts or opinions about anything. My mind felt completely blank."

There are many causes for Dissociation/Derealisation. According to the mental health charity Mind, "you might experience dissociation as a symptom of a mental health problem... or as a side effect of some drugs, medication, coming off medication and alcohol. The use of cannabis or hallucinogens in particular can trigger Dissociation/Derealisation and lead to depression, self-harm, low self-esteem and such physical symptoms of blurry vision and visual snow."

And like Jack, James suffered from terrible anxiety and thoughts of suicide. But his story had a happy ending. He found a therapist who helped him understand the trauma that had created his Dissociation and through treatment managed to get back his old self.

So if Jack was suffering from Depersonalisation why didn't he get treatment for that? Because Jack was never diagnosed as suffering from Dissociation by his doctor, his therapist, his psychiatrist or mental health workers. They thought the problem was down to depression, acute anxiety and his use of drugs.

The only person who thought Jack was suffering from Dissociation was Jack. (He used the term "Depersonalisation", which is one of the various forms of dissociation.) "I have experienced continually increasing levels of Depersonalisation since the age of 18 (2004)".

In October 2015 I tried to get Jack into the Depersonalisation Clinic at the South London and Maudsley NHS trust but Jack's local Clinical Commissioning Group refused to pay for his treatment and it was too high a price for his mum and me to pay. Now I dread to think what the price was for Jack. That said, there is no guarantee that had he got treatment there he would have been saved. He had to stop taking drugs if he were to ever have a chance of changing his life.

• • •

By now drugs stop being recreational and have become an obsession. He's not a junkie, he's a stoner. Junkies have only one love: heroin. Stoners are promiscuous; they love getting high by any means possible. Stoners are always stoned. Or looking to get stoned. Or talking about getting stoned. The world of the stoner revolves around not getting high, but getting "wasted". "Fucked". "Trashed". For stoners like Jack drugs are not a means of expanding your mind; they're a means of escaping it. Hence the expression "getting out of your head."

When Jack was stoned, all the sound and fury raging inside his mind would go on mute. He was self-medicating, but treating the problem with his problem. Drugs gave Jack purpose and, at first, pleasure. They made this socially anxious boy socially brave and indifferent to the bullshit of other people and the hassles of life. And if he took too much dope, what did it matter? Being fucked-up allowed him the luxury of not giving a damn; and for Lost Boys like Jack, that's called freedom.

Close friends notice that Jack is changing for the worse. They feel they're losing their lovable, sweet Jack to crazy, out-of-control drug obsessed Stoner Jack. His drug use causes friction and conflict with friends. Jack later admits that, "My obsession with drugs resulted in some very ugly falling outs with people closest to me."

People like his ex-girlfriend Bianca who got so fed-up with Jack constantly nagging her for weed, she decided to end their relationship. Drugs killed his relationship with his girlfriend Melissa. (She was in love with Jack, but Jack was in love with drugs.) Drugs also cost him his friendship with Jake. Drugs damaged his relationship with his mother and me. And drugs damaged his relationship with himself. He hated what he called the "mentally fucked drug-crazed nutter" he'd become.

He knew what drugs were doing to him, to his life. In July 2014 two social workers with the Camden and Islington Mental Health Assessment and Advice Teams wrote to Jack's GP with their assessment of Jack. They made this telling point. "Jack understands that his drug use had led to social issues, including housing concerns – inability to maintain stable accommodation, couch surfing and squatting; sustain employment due to difficulty interacting with others, poor concentration and memory making it difficult to follow step-by-step duties and difficulty with organising self and fulfilling requirements to maintain welfare benefits, e.g. attending appointments on time."

Jack understood what the doctors were telling him. He knew he was screwing up his life with drugs. But Jack didn't care. I once asked him why, when he knew that drugs were messing up his life, did he carry on taking them?

And he told me: "once you decide to kill yourself, you might as well get wasted."

I tried to convince him that "getting wasted" was one reason he was trying to kill himself. But it was impossible to persuade Jack of just about anything. He had these deep convictions – founded on I don't know what – that he was right and you were wrong about everything. His reasoning defied logic, his facts were fictions.

I would patiently make out a case for why he could stop taking drugs and change his life and even have a happy life – and he'd follow my argument, nodding along in agreement and saying "yeah, I see that" and I would think I've got you…yes by the sheer force of my Socratic reasoning I have you! And so I'd finish with the irrefutable conclusion that he could not deny.

Me: Therefore, is it not possible that you could change too?

Jack: Yeah, everything you say is true. Change is possible.

And I'm thinking: Yes! Yes! I've done it!

And then Jack says: It's just not possible for me.

Once again, I have banged my head against the brick wall that is Jack.

• • •

Drugs damaged not only his mind but his moral compass. The old Jack had a very clear sense of right and wrong. He believed that you had to treat people with respect and fairness. But this Stoner Jack doesn't care about right and wrong and being a good guy. He hits the streets and begs for money, claiming he wants to buy food when really he wants to buy drugs. He tells me that he sells fake drugs and when I ask how he could do that Jack just says, "they deserve it". I'm even more shocked when he tells me a plan to sell Nembutal to people like him who want to die. He starts shoplifting – and gets caught. And he feels no sense of shame when he steals and sells a friend's guitar to score dope.

• • •

I try to get Jack to go to Narcotics Anonymous. Eventually, he agrees to go to a meeting and I'm hopeful this could be the turning point in the Jack story: the first step to recovery.

On his return I ask: how did it go?

Jack: Waste of fucking time, he says.

Me: What? How can you dismiss it after just one meeting?

Jack: Dad, those people are such depressed losers! All they do is sit around moaning about their lives.

Me: Jack, you're wrong. NA changes people's lives. It can help you change your life.

Jack: No thanks.

Me: What? You'd rather just sit on your arse all day and get wasted?

Jack: Indeed I do!

Oh, Jack. I give up…

• • •

Every parent with a Jack of their own will know that exasperated cry of: *I give up*! You have reached that point of emotional exhaustion and you say to yourself: there's no point in carrying on. I quit.

You know with absolute certainty there's *nothing* you can do. You've tried everything and everything has failed. No, it's time to let them go and if they screw up their lives, well…that's their choice. What can you do? You have to admit defeat and give up.

Life Lesson Number Seven: *Give Up Giving Up*

There's no such thing as giving up; your love and anxiety won't let you. The best thing to do when you feel like giving up is wait a day. A week. And start over again. Nothing is more impossible than watching your child or your loved one screwing up their life and doing nothing.

• • •

Before Jack's death I'd never questioned my liberal belief that recreational drugs were a valid and safe form of pleasure. People like me who as teenagers growing up in the late sixties and early seventies saw drug usage as a harmless rite of passage; a phase of youthful experimentation and exploration that reflected an admirable openness to life. Back then any talk of the damage that drugs could do was dismissed by us as "tabloid hysteria". Had we not been there and smoked/sniffed/snorted that? And look at what nice, sensible bourgeois adults we turned out to be. So when it was the turn of our children to experience drugs there was no need to worry. They'd be fine.

We thought we were so smart and cool about drugs, but we were just naive, arrogant and ignorant. I have no regrets about my own drug usage – not too many – and I don't believe I could have stopped Jack from experimenting with drugs. But I could have warned him about the dangerous side effects that drug usage can have on certain people like him. There's now plenty of medical evidence that shows that the regular use of drugs like ecstasy and weed – in particular skunk – can leave the user feeling exactly the kind of emotional and social detachment that Jack experienced.

• • •

I would lecture Jack about the need for him to stop taking drugs, and Jack would lecture me about the need to start taking drugs.

I would say to him: drugs are fucking-you up!

And he would say to me: dad, you're fucked-up already. Drugs could help you.

In an email to me Jack wrote:

"What I suggest you do is find some way to truly channel the anxiety, stress and unhappiness inside yourself so that it doesn't play such a dominant role in your relationships. I do this through intoxicants. Maybe you should do the same too? I can never understand your constant reluctance to get fucked-up, as – no offence pal – you need it more than literally anyone else I know."

And just as I was always offering to buy Jack self-help books, Jack was always offering to buy me drugs.

Jack: Would you like some weed? Acid? Crack? I can get whatever you want!

"No, thank you!

"Ok. I was just trying to be nice."

It was his way of impressing me. Of showing how cool and well-connected he was. I think he felt disappointed that I refused to take drugs with him. He knew that I'd taken acid and smoked pot in my teens and done plenty of coke in my thirties. He also knew that I had got stoned with my boho parents back in the late sixties. So why not now? Why not with him? He always wanted us to get high together.

A typical Jack invite went like this:

Jack: Come on man. Let's do some weed and watch *The Texas Chainsaw Massacre*!

Me: Jack, as tempting as that is, I think I'm gonna pass on that one.

Jack: C'mon dad. You never want to hang out and get high.

He was right. But there were times when I was tempted. Times when I thought: *oh fuck it, let's just get high and have some fun together*! I'd tell myself you're always acting like Jack's therapist/ confessor/parole officer – you're always doing the concerned dad thing. Why not be a buddy for once? You can have one little joint with him. (Frankly, he's so fucked-up already, what difference will one joint make?) I could say: come on son, roll one up and let's rip! Let's just chill and hang, father and son, smashed out of our brains together! We'll gorge on ice cream and horror movies and play each other our favourite records all night long – fuck that job interview early tomorrow morning! Hey, we could get really stoned and watch *Postman Pat* or do some acid and watch *The Clangers* – those guys are on acid already! Remember we used to watch them when you were a small boy? Fuck it! Let's do it! C'mon Jack, skin 'em up and I'll put out a line. Acccccccid!

But I never did because I wanted to be a responsible parent and that meant I could not condone Jack using drugs; as if my approval or disapproval would have any influence on him. My Just Say No To Jack position had no practical application; it just made me feel better about myself.

I Love You, Man

Jack comes over to my place on Boxing Day 2014. We're in the kitchen making tea and small talk when suddenly he says something that he's never said to me before: he says he loves me.

And then he tries to hug me and our shoulders collide in an awkward half-hug, half rugby block embrace.

I think that most dads would have replied with something like, "thanks!" or, "I love you too!"

Not me. I say: are you on drugs?

No, he says. Honest.

Jack tells me I'm a really good guy who has his flaws. He tells me again that he loves me and once again I ask if he's on drugs?

No, he says. Honest!

So, how's it going? he asks. Tell me about your life.

This is weird. We only really talk about his life and his problems. I feel awkward. Confused. What am I meant to say? I could fob him off with the standard life's fine, so-so, up-and-down etc. But he's really trying to reach out to me, he wants to know about me so I should make an effort. I tell him that yes, I'm disappointed with the way my life has turned out – like a million other men – but I make the best of things. And in some ways…

But Jack is not listening. He goes to my laptop and starts to play George Michael's 'Careless Whisper' on Spotify. "This is such a beautiful song," he says in a dreamy, wistful way – and I know for certain Jack is high on drugs.

"Yeah, I took some acid this morning," he casually confesses.

I feel disappointed. For a minute there I thought we were having a real father and son moment and that the battle between us had stopped. We had dropped our guards and were, for once, being open and honest with each other.

For a minute there, I thought he loved me.

14

Living With Jack

"I live with a large, inert lump at the centre of my living room. My lump is called Jack. It just sits there doing nothing. All day. His depression spreads through the flat like damp; the undertow of his inertia threatens to take me under with him."

Diary note from 2012.

That's how I remember living with Jack. I can see him now – sitting up on the sofa-bed watching his laptop; bed and boy dominate my room. Jack could never be bothered to put the once white duvet cover on his duvet. He just drapes it around his naked shoulders and what with his self-harming scars on his arms and his pale skinny body, he looks like someone who was wrapped-up in a very large and soiled bandage waiting for medical attention.

My living room is usually a tidy, calm and orderly space. (Someone once described it as resembling a Mayfair doctor's waiting room.) But when Jack comes to stay – even just for one night – the room is instantly transformed to a state of total squalor. Black dustbin bags full of Jack's stuff zigzag across the room; some are open and spewing out their contents – silver packets of medication, phone chargers, guitars strings, socks, copies of *Kerrang*! – onto the carpet. His bass guitar has been planted into my armchair while his grimy hoody, his split trainers, ripped jeans and his soiled duffel bag are discarded on the floor and droop from side tables and chairs.

Usually on my small writing table in the corner there's just one book, one notebook, one pencil. I keep it simple. It's the perfect spot for morning coffee and creative contemplation. It's my special spot. Now it's Jack's spot; his dumping ground for Jack clutter: paperback biographies of damaged or dead rock stars; more tea cups, pizza boxes, printouts of doctor appointments, letters from social security, scrawled reminders by Jack to Jack which will be forgotten by Jack.

A Day In The Life Of Jack And Me

It could be 2 or 3 in the afternoon. Outside is sunshine or maybe rain; it doesn't matter to Jack. He has another busy day ahead doing nothing.

There was a time when Jack did make attempts at finding work. He found jobs and quickly lost them. He mostly went in for tele-sales, which involved calling up people who did not want you to call them and sell them something they did not want to buy. Jack always insisted that he was really good at selling and had a bright future in the business – this despite the fact that over a five-year period he never made one sale. Not one.

But since his brain "broke" in 2012 he says he can't work. So he's still in bed or he went out to sign on to the dole and came home and went back to bed. Bed is his comfort zone, his sanctuary from the world and from himself. He just sits there; a Lost Boy soothed and sustained by the drip-feed of distraction coming from his laptop.

Jack doesn't mean to cause problems or be a pain. And there are times when he sees me doing some cleaning around the flat and asks if I need a hand?

And I think: No, I need you to get your shit together. The truth is: I want the lump out of my living room. But the lump – my lump – needs my care. My sofa. My love.

I accepted the fact that Jack was very depressed and prone to anxiety but I also wondered if his condition was made worse – or at least sustained – by flaws in his character. He was disabled by indolence. The very idea of having character flaws sounds something Victorian and moralistic, and that makes us moderns nervous. The role of character has little place in modern day thinking about the origins or treatment of mental health problems. I didn't believe that all he had to do was stop whining and pull himself together; but I did think he had to make some effort to get his life back on track.

Certain character traits equip us to deal with the problems caused by mental health – or just the adverse conditions of life in general – better than others. Perhaps this explains why certain people can push through and overcome their depression and others can't. One depressed person will sit in bed all day while another will force themselves to go and exercise. It seemed to be that Jack's laziness was so great that he couldn't be "arsed" – to use a key Jack word – to save his own life.

The thing about living with the depressed is this; they're so damn depressing to live with! At least with bi-polar people – or so I imagine – you get dramatic mood swings: they're up, they're down. But depression is just flat, monochromatic, monotonous. Dull. As the writer Tim Lott puts it, depression is "a deeply unattractive illness to be around." To outsiders it looks more like "malingering, bad temper and ugly behaviour" than a real disease. "And who can empathise with such unattractive traits?" asks Lott.

Sometimes on good days I tell myself: be patient with Jack, don't get so cross, show him more understanding and kindness. But on bad days I yell at him: *Why don't you get off your arse and get a job? Do something! Go for a run! Work in the local charity shop! You can't just sit around all day watching YouTube and listening to that depressing music of yours.*

And sometimes on good days Jack would say, "yeah you're right. I'll find something to do."

But on bad days he'd yell at me, his face all red and his fists clenched in frustration and say through clenched teeth, "You don't understand…you don't get it, my brain is fucking broken!"

● ● ●

I would go out in the morning and return late in the afternoon, only to find Jack exactly as I'd left him; still in bed before his laptop screen. The only sign of any change or the passage of time was the appearance of new mugs of half drunken tea, the proliferation of flap-jack wrappers, and the empty bottles of Mountain Dew by his bedside.

I wasn't the only one to experience the horrors of living with the lump. My friend the writer Michele Kirsch who knew Jack as a baby gave him a place to stay when he was homeless in 2014. She did so much to take care of him and loved him dearly, but Michele told me after his death that his presence in her small flat drove her nuts. The way he just, "lay there in bed all day saying how everyone *sucked* and everything *sucked* and I'd be working all day like a dog and giving him all my money!" Eventually, she had to ask Jack to leave due to his drug use.

Everyone – his mum, me, his friends, girlfriends, kind strangers – eventually had to ask Jack to leave. He broke your rules, crossed your lines, ignored your barriers and polite requests because he did not recognize your right to have them. You were just being uptight or neurotic; the best thing you could do was, "chill out!"

Dinner With Jack

And when we'd sit down to dinner, it was like the dinners we'd had when he was a small boy and his mum had first left the family home. This time around we didn't have *The Simpsons* to distract us, so we filled the silence with small talk that usually went something like this:

Me: So how's it going?

Jack: Yeah, all good.

Me: What you been doing today?

Jack: This and that. You?

Me: You know. Same old, same old.

Jack: Yeah…

And then the small talk would become no talk and out came the laptops.

• • •

I'm no foodie nor do I claim to be a great cook, but I would make an effort to try and cook a nice meal for us. But no matter what I served – a chicken curry or his beloved spaghetti bolognese – Jack would take whatever was on his plate, drench it in ketchup, scoop it up and spread it out between two hunks of big, thick white bread and quickly woof it down and wash it away with his beloved Mountain Dew.

"Great meal dad, cheers!"

I'd smile and shake my head in disbelief.

"Whaat?" asked Jack.

Dinners with Jack always left me feeling low. It wasn't just because of what he did with my food or what we didn't talk about; it was my life that was the problem. Here I was about to turn sixty, single – I had broken up with Alice – and living with my son, the lump. This wasn't exactly the sort of life I imagined I'd have one day. I thought there would be a wife, a couple of kids and friends sitting around a big table having dinner together. There would be laughs and loud conversations just like my family had. But no. It was just Jack and just me.

Maybe you're thinking: *why didn't you just invite somebody over to have dinner with you and Jack?*

Believe me, I tried. Jack hated it when I said we had a guest for dinner. "Fuck, why did you do that? You know I can't handle being with people!" I once invited this really cool young friend of mine called Holly Groom to have dinner with Jack and me. She had tats, piercings and knew all about indie bands. I knew she and Jack would get on great, but when she arrived Jack freaked out and ran and hid in another room until she left.

Jack, what the hell was that? You promised you'd stay and have dinner with Holly.

"I can't be with people!" he told me, "They look into my eyes and see that I'm dead inside. It's unbearable!"

"Jack, it's just dinner! Bit of chat. Some nice grub. A few laughs. What's the big deal?"

"No man, you don't understand."

"No Jack, you don't understand."

Even at the time I could see that these were just projections of his intense social anxiety. The fact is, nobody saw Jack as the dead-inside-drooling-zombie Jack claimed everyone saw; they saw a sweet and charming young man. On one occasion a teenage son of a friend came around and I noticed that he and Jack were talking about bands and guitars with total ease. When later I pointed this out, Jack seemed to be taken by surprise; for a second his whole brain damage thing didn't fit the facts. But he quickly recovered saying, "I was just on autopilot. Really, I had nothing to say."

• • •

Jack and I used to have fun together when he was a small boy – but then along came adolescence and everything changed. We could never find that shared passion or interest in something – films, music, sport, cars – by which a father and son can build a bond beyond mere biology or obligation. These common interests give you something to talk about at dinner time and something to do together on wet Sunday afternoons.

I always thought that such a bond could be built around a mutual love of pop music. When he was a kid he enjoyed the records I played him: 'The Monster Mash', 'Bridget The Midget', 'School's Out' and 'Run Rabbit Run' (the definitive version by Pinky and Perky). So I was looking forward to the day I would introduce him to more grown-up stuff like The Beatles, The Who, Dylan, Hendrix – and he would be wowed and take a nerdy interest in bands of the 60s, keeping elaborate lists of groups, their changing line-ups and dates of album releases. Jack would look at me with wide-eyed wonder and ask, "Dad, what was it like seeing The Doors live at The Roundhouse?"

"Well son, funny you should ask…" and I would regale him with stories of great gigs – Hendrix at the Saville Theatre in 68, the bands I saw at Woodstock, Dylan at the Isle of Wight – and he would look at me with awe instead of the bored expression he usually gave my great rock gig reminiscences.

I knew that as a teenager he was at an age when pop music is a means of carving out your own identity and not a way to bond with your dad. But why, I thought, couldn't he do both? There was no rule that said you had to hate the music that your parents loved, was there? (That was a very dated, 1960s generation-gap notion of music.) I loved listening to the music my parents played – jazz, show tunes, Lotte Lenya, Miles Davis. And I'd often heard people, especially musicians, talking about how they were introduced to music by listening to the music their parents loved. So why not us?

By his early twenties Jack was obsessed with music and when he taught himself to play bass and lead guitar I thought, Great! We can jam together! I knew all the basic blues and rock chords – and songs – that every guitarist starts off with – every guitarist but Jack. I would play a basic 12-bar blues riff and Jack would play a basic psychotic fast and furious trash metal lead guitar. It was an incongruous combination that produced a hideous cacophony. We were just speaking two very different languages and soon quit playing together owing to creative differences, as they say.

What's more, Jack had no interest in his dad's kind of music. I tried Dylan, the Beatles, the Stones on him and each time the Jack verdict was the same: "Not my sort of thing," he'd say. Not my sort of thing was Jack's polite way of saying: *Dad, this music is fucking shit! How can you like this crap?*

I tried to win him over with the harder stuff like the MC5 and Iggy and the Stooges. They played the kind of primordial punkish rock that I thought he would love, but they too were not his sort of thing. I was on the verge of giving up when one day I discovered a band he loved called the Murder Dolls – an American glam-punk band – who I could tell were influenced in looks and style by one of my favourite bands, The New York Dolls. Eureka, I thought! At last I had a band with a song – Jet Boy – that I knew Jack would love. He had to love it! It was fast and hard just like his beloved Murder Dolls. I played it to him at full volume. The furniture shook, but Jack was unmoved.

"Not my sort of thing," said Jack.

"But…but how can you not love Jet Boy – it's a classic!"

"Dunno. It's just…"

"Yeah, I know! It's not your sort of thing. But nothing I like is your sort of thing."

"Dad, no need to get all pissy just 'cause I didn't like your record!"

"It's not that. It's your attitude…"

"What?"

"Oh, never mind" I said.

• • •

To be fair, I couldn't really appreciate his type of music either. He loved Marilyn Manson, who I dismissed as "Alice Cooper for morons." When I called his beloved Insane Clown Posse – a violent rock/rap group – Insane Clown Pussies to piss him off, Jack just smiled and said, "Good one dad!"

Then after a brief love of Eminem – who I kind of liked – Jack got into the real psychotic trash/nu-metal stuff like Slipknot, Korn, Bile and System of Down. Jack played me his favourite Slipknot track, *People=Shit* and I instantly got a headache. These bands were faster, louder and more aggressive than the heavy metal bands of my youth like Led Zeppelin and Black Sabbath. This was heavy metal gone mad; melodies were mashed into audio sludge; lyrics were screamed over frenzied rhythms and spewed into the listener's ears. In honour of Phil Spector's Wall of Sound, I called it the Wall of Vomit and told Jack so.

Jack said: Who's Phil Spector?

And so music – which should have brought us together – actually pushed us apart into two mutually hostile camps: my Dad Rock Vs his Psychotic Metal. Of course I blamed Jack for this. It was, for me, another example of his refusal to give anything a chance be it music, art or travel. He had no curiosity about life or culture and this only exacerbated my disappointment in the whole experience of fatherhood.

Life Lesson Eight: *Listen To Their Music*

(Christ, I sound like the Doobie Brothers!) I never really tried to listen to the bands that Jack loved; just like I never gave his beloved video games a chance. In my own way I was as closed-off to new things as Jack was.

You may hate their music, but you have to listen to it. Yes, that terrible racket, that awful, instant, migraine assault on your ears is touching the heart and soul of your child. It's speaking to them and for them; articulating all of the dark rage and hurt that they hide from you. It's not easy listening to that kind of music, but after Jack died I started listening to bands like Slipknot, Korn, Type O Negative and guess what: I got it! I'm not claiming I love it, but I saw and heard what Jack saw and heard and we could have shared that.

But no, dad had to stick with his little precious canon of old rock classics and complain that Jack never gave anything a chance.

I Hear Jack…

I hear Jack in the kitchen making tea. I can hear the kettle boil and it clicks off and then I hear Jack crying. He just breaks down and cries. I don't know if he has a reason – or a thousand-and-one reasons. I've not heard him cry since he was a kid.

I go to him and shyly put a hand on his shoulder and softly say, "You ok Jack?"

"Yeah yeah. All good" he says.

"Want to talk?"

"Naah. Thanks."

"Ok," I say. "If you wanna talk, I'm here."

"Ok. Cheers dad."

Jack Hears Me…

"What's wrong dad?" Jack asks.

Jack has caught me in a moment of despair. I'm in the kitchen, head slumped in hands.

Nothing, I say.

But Jack's not fooled. He prods me a bit more and out it comes: all my pent-up despair about him, his condition and nothing ever changing.

"I don't know Jack. Sometimes I think, this is it. Forever. You're fucked. I'm fucked. Nothing will ever change."

And Jack says: "I'm sorry to put you through this…really sorry."

Suddenly, he starts to slap and then punch himself in the face. "I'm a fucking idiot (slap!)…I'm a fucking useless, shit person. (whack!) Useless-shit-person! (slap!) I'm so sorry."

"Jack! Stop that! Please."

And I tell myself: well done Super Dad – you've just given him another reason for suicide.

Not My Sort Of Thing Part Two: Books

The same thing happened with books as happened with music. I'd always hoped that Jack would share my love of books. I got that from my mother when I was a teenager. She gave me a copy of *Catcher in The Rye*, and it was as if a missing bit of me was put in place. I gave Jack that same battered Penguin copy of *Catcher in The Rye* my mother had given me.

"You'll love this book!" I said to him.

My Jack book fantasy went like this. He'd read *Catcher in The Rye* and naturally he'd love it and ask me for other great books to read. Soon we'd be off to the Hay-On-Wye Literary Festival together, discussing – over dinner – the state of the American novel and going to see Martin Amis in conversation at Waterstones together. And on grey, wet Sunday afternoons we would browse second-hand book shops on Charing Cross Road together, sharing our treasures over coffee at the London Review of Books coffee shop in Bloomsbury. And Jack's first novel would be dedicated to guess who?

But he didn't like *Catcher in The Rye*.

"Not my sort of thing," he said.

Of course, I took this personally. In rejecting a book that had meant so much to me Jack was, in my mind, rejecting me. It was more proof of our estrangement from each other. Here I was trying to be a good dad and all I got for my efforts was: *not really my thing, Dad*. I'd sulked for a while and then I'd try another of my other favourite writers on him, like Orwell, Huxley or Dostoyevsky. And each time we'd always go through the same ritual of his grateful receiving of the book – "thanks for that!" – followed by the inevitable rejection and return of the book with: "not my sort of thing."

But I did not give up hope. I used to see Jack hanging out at my local library. (He went there on days when he had nowhere to go and nothing to do.) I hoped that while there he would stumble upon a book that would change his life. (Maybe even save his life?) Jack, I imagined, would come back from the library with that life-transforming book and say, "Dad! I've found this *amazing book*!" and for the next few days instead of sitting like a zombie in front of his laptop, Jack would devour that book, and that book would devour Jack and he would bloom into a happy man.

He never found that book, but I did. One day while browsing around the library shelves I discovered *Reasons to Live* by Matt Haig. It's Haig's brilliant account of his battle with depression. What grabbed my attention and got me hopeful was a chapter that began, "I remember the day the old me died" – which sounded exactly like Jack talking. Haig's chapters were short and the prose easy and enjoyable to read. It was funny, moving and wise. I could now forget about all those earnest, self-help titles I kept thrusting onto Jack: this *had* to be the book that would make a difference. So I took it out and gave it to Jack.

A week later I asked him what he thought of *Reasons to Live*.

"Yeah, it's good," he said.

"You didn't read it, did you?"

"Sorry. It's not my…"

"Ok! Yeah, got it!"

After that one, I just gave up.

What If?

Living with Jack meant living with the possibility of one day finding his dead body. In the morning I would go into the living room with a cup of tea to wake Jack up and I would look at his still body and wonder: is he asleep or is he dead?

This is not a great way to start your day.

And sometimes I would come home from an evening out, climb the stairs and wonder: has he done it? If I go into the living room, what will I find? Will I look out the window and see Jack hanging down from the terrace above, suspended in mid-air like an apparition?

Hanging remains the most popular form of suicide for men in the UK. To find a loved one hanging is, I imagine, the worst discovery of them all. It's the most cinematic form of self-execution; a horror movie moment that lasts forever.

What makes death by hanging so shocking is the juxtaposition between the stuff of nightmares and the normality of everyday domesticity. The body hangs in the air – at first glance, appearing to defy gravity – surrounded by earthbound things: tea cups, flowers, a clock, a bed, books, a dirty hairbrush.

There were periods of life with Jack when the immediate threat of suicide would get left behind by the passing of days. You are inoculated against the threat by routine. Normality takes over. Jack's talk of suicide sounds just like talk. I can relax.

And then Jacks tells me how a few days ago he tried to hang himself from the back of the door – my sitting room door! – with a plastic bag over his face but the hook on the back of the door came out and he fell to his knees. So I returned to that state of suspension between the improbability of Jack actually killing himself and the possibility that Jack just might do it.

Rowing With Jack

When we lived together Jack and I used to row about everything: big and small. We had rows about him putting the recycled rubbish in the wrong bin and rows about cheese crackers (he ate them all!) and ice cream (while stoned he ate the whole tub.) We had rows about his failure to pay back money he borrowed from me. We rowed about the lousy job he did cleaning my windows and forgetting to take out the rubbish on a Thursday evening – yes the same row we had years ago! We rowed about rowing. I said it was his fault we rowed because he never did the things I asked him; he said it was my fault because I didn't ask nicely and that I yelled and bossed him around.

"You're like a Nazi guard at a concentration camp", he once complained, and you can imagine the row that followed that remark.

We even had a terrible row about a toothbrush. My toothbrush. Jack kept using my toothbrush, even though he had his own toothbrush. For me, this was a line-in-the-sand issue. Jack had to learn to respect me and my wishes and that meant respecting my toothbrush. Yes, it was a small thing but if I couldn't get Jack to accommodate this small thing, then I could make no demands at all; and that way led to anarchy. Today my toothbrush, tomorrow my scented baby wipes and god knows what else! I realise this sounds like a crazy man talking. I was. I am.

There came the day, when after repeated warnings, he did it again: he used *my* toothbrush and I went ballistic and shouted: *I ask only one thing of you while you stay here: don't use my fucking toothbrush!* I then thrust my toothbrush close to his face as if it were a switchblade. "This is my toothbrush," I said, "It's a toothbrush with a red handle. Got that? Now this is your toothbrush," and here I held up his toothbrush, "You will notice that its handle is green and if you look carefully you will see that the bristles are long in the back and short in the front. My bristles are one size only. Can you really not tell the difference between the two toothbrushes?"

I forgot, he said. Sorry.

That should have been the end of that. But there was not the appropriate note of contrition and sorrow in his voice. On the contrary, I sensed that Jack didn't care about using my toothbrush. Worse still, he did not recognize the legitimacy of my toothbrush demands. I knew what he was thinking: *what's this crazy fucker going on about?*

"One small thing! Just one small thing I ask of you and you can't be arsed to do that!" I continued. On and on I ranted at him about his selfishness, his thoughtlessness and his carelessness. I even said that unless we can resolve the toothbrush issue he would have to leave and go live somewhere else. "I can't live like this!" I said sounding like a man on the verge of a nervous breakdown.

Jack looked puzzled and said, "Man…It's just a toothbrush! Why are you freaking-out? I'm depressed and I'm suicidal – and all you care about is your fucking toothbrush!"

He had a point. I now look back at the toothbrush row with a sense of shame and disbelief. I actually fought a battle – one rooted in reason and righteousness – and inflicted pain on my poor son in the name of a toothbrush. That row and all our rows were so pointless and yet so inevitable. This is what happens when a messy boy with a messed-up mind lives with a melancholic dad who wants a tidy flat and a tidy life and for no one to touch his toothbrush.

• • •

Jack and I had rows, and then we had rages. Some trivial incident would trigger an ancient hurt, inflame an old wound and before we knew it Jack and I were engaged in a bloody father-son gladiatorial battle where the idea was to inflict as much emotional hurt on the other as possible.

Me: Oh you useless fuck! You just sit around doing nothing all day! Your life is shit because you can't be arsed to try and make it any better!

Jack: Dad, you need to do something about your sad, depressed life. You need to find some joy in your life, bro.

Me: Listen bro, you're the one with the shit life! My life is fine, thank you very much!

Jack: Then why are you so depressed all the time?

Me: Why are you?

Jack knew how to press my hurt buttons. And the most painful of them all was the one labelled: *You Are a Shit Dad*.

Jack: You're a shit dad. You've always been a shit dad to me. You're always angry and shouting at people.

Me: Really? You've not exactly been my dream son either. And you shout at people too. You're always getting into fights. So please don't lecture me about getting angry!

I should have seen the funny side of Jack lecturing me about the failure of my life, but I didn't. And on a few occasions – maybe two or three – the adrenalin of our anger would be so high we'd go from yelling at each other to the threat of physical combat. He would step up to me, close, the way a boxer faces off to his opponent in a ring at the beginning of a fight. And I would step up to him. He'd try and stare me down and I could see his clenched fists by his side and hear the pulleys and levers of his self-control creaking into action. He wanted to hit me. "Go on, do it," I'd say. "Fucking do it!"

Did I want to hit him? Yes and no. (Thank God no blows were ever exchanged.) I had no desire to hurt or damage him physically. I wanted to shake and slap him out of his inertia and get him to fight back. Even if it meant fighting me, at least that would be a sign of some drive towards life, some will to survival. (And after our fight, I imagined, we would shake hands, declare no hard feelings and go off to the pub and get pissed together. A ridiculous fantasy, I know.) We once had a very ugly encounter that involved me shoving him and he shoving me back and suddenly we were wrestling. I held him down and he struggled to get free. It looked bad from the outside, but it was mostly a lot of theatrical huffing and puffing. He wasn't physically hurt but he was humiliated by this incident.

Where did all this crazy anger – his anger, my anger – come from? Years of disappointment, frustration, resentment and hurt had festered beneath the surface – all that swirling shit in the sewer of the subconscious – would burst forth in volcanic eruptions. I wanted to help this damaged boy of mine. I wanted to love him and make his life worthwhile; and look at what I was doing! Adding to his hurt, increasing his damage. Why couldn't I see what was so obvious: that he lashed out at me because I had hurt him. Life had hurt him. Why couldn't I have been a grown-up, been a Good Dad and said, "Lets stop trying to wound each other and try and look after each other?"

That's what a better man and a better dad would have said. But all my good intentions got blown away in the explosion of my anger. I was angry at him for denying me the chance of being the father I wanted to be: The Fun Dad. The Proud Dad. The Good Dad. But he would never listen to me, never take my suggestions as to what he should do. I wanted to save him, but he refused to be saved by me or anyone. He would just go on and on screwing-up forever. And that made me angry when it should have made me kinder, softer and more patient.

The irony here is that he was giving me the chance to be that dad I wanted to be – the kind, patient and loving dad. And yes there were moments when I was that dad, but not enough.

Life Lesson Number Nine: *You Are Part Of The Problem*

The great mistake made by parents who have children like Jack is to think that the child is the one with all the problems. I assumed that all I had to do was just sort Jack out and everything would be fine. But I couldn't sort him out, because I hadn't sorted out myself. We parents are so focused on the problems of our children that we lose sight of the fact that we are part of the problem.

We want to save them and so we turn to medical or psychotherapeutic solutions. But we need to work on ourselves as well. We are angry, hurt, confused, perplexed and afraid. We are full of love and hate – and yet we need to cultivate a degree of patience, kindness, care and support for our problematic child that seems impossible. We have to be the parents we've always dreamed of being, but have never managed. We have to up our game as parents and as individuals and if we don't we can lose someone we love. So we try and fail. And try again. And no, I'm not going to quote the Samuel Beckett line which is actually a life lesson for highbrows who look down on life lessons!

· · ·

There were times when these rows got too much and I would just throw him out of my flat. "That's it!" I would bark. "I've had enough of you. Just get your shit together and get out. *Now*!"

And silently Jack would begin the slow process of collecting his stuff – his laptop, mobile phone, various chargers, a copy of *Kerrang!* magazine and a few items of clothing – and push it all into his black rucksack and one black dustbin bag. During this packing up there was always that little gap of silence, when the shouting had stopped, the rage had subsided and there was a chance for us to make up.

I could have said sorry.

He could have said sorry.

And we could have had tea and talked it over and come to some sort of understanding.

But we said nothing.

I knew what he was feeling: Hurt. Anger. And a bit confused: why had his dad done this? Why had his dad thrown him out onto the streets with nowhere to go, no money and no credit on his phone? And it's fucking raining! What a complete cunt my dad is.

But Jack had too much pride to show any pain or complain about his treatment. He just stayed silent and packed up his stuff.

And during the ensuing quiet I would feel a spasm of guilt and had to remind myself that Jack was impossible to live with. You don't believe me? Ask anyone who ever lived with Jack. His mother tried to provide a home for him – but she found it too much. Two friends of mine, who had known Jack as a small boy, had tried to take him in and look after him – but eventually they had to ask him to leave. Some hippies who gave him shelter were so freaked out by his drug dealing they asked him to leave. Jack even proved too hard to live with for a group of anarchist squatters in Hackney – they too kicked him out.

My indignation was now reignited. I'd follow him down the stairs. "We're finished, you ungrateful shit! And don't come around here anymore and don't call me. I've had it with you."

Jack stayed silent.

I would wait for the sound of the front door being shut. I always expected him to give it a defiant fuck-you-dad slamming of the door; but he'd quietly shut it. From a window I'd watch him out on the darkening street looking around, wondering where to go. It's hard to know where to go when you have nowhere to go. But Jack, like some bird driven by instinct, would suddenly trudge off with an air of purpose to God knows where: a park, a pavement or maybe a friend's sofa? How lonely and hurt he must have felt.

Poor Jack. All fucked-up and nowhere to go.

He had lost his parents and his friends. He was now homeless. Years later Jack wrote of this time when he got kicked out, "And that's when things got really dark."

15

We Are Family

I had kicked Jack out of my flat and right into homelessness. How could a supposedly loving and caring parent do that? But that's what we loving and caring parents sometimes do. No doubt some caring parents call that cruel; others call it Tough Love.

The logic of Tough Love goes like this: after a certain age our child has to take responsibility for their choices in life. And that means accepting the consequences of your actions. You smoke dope and miss an appointment that will get you a Job Seekers Allowance? Ok. But don't ask mummy or daddy for money; pay the price. If you refuse to play by the rules of the house you're staying in – don't complain when you're kicked out and find yourself homeless; pay the price. You're hungry? Tired? Lonely? Afraid? Tough. I won't help you. It's time you helped yourself.

The thing about Tough Love is that it's tough to do. It goes against every caring and loving instinct a parent has. There's nothing harder than watching someone you love screw-up their life – and do nothing about it. But what else could I do?

With kids like Jack, parents and friends eventually experience a kind of care fatigue. All your efforts to help have ended in failure; every new beginning ends in going back to old ways. And after a few years of nothing ever changing, you're left feeling exhausted. The hope you once had is replaced by an overwhelming sense of futility.

You no longer wonder what you can do. You wonder: why bother doing it?

I tried to get Jack to get on the Islington council waiting list for housing. I knew it would take forever, but it would pay off one day.

But Jack couldn't be bothered. I told him to find and keep the numbers of emergency shelters and hostels for the homeless at hand so he would never have to sleep on the streets. But Jack couldn't be bothered. A friend of mine tried to help Jack by getting him accommodation via a charity that helped recovering addicts.

"No thanks", said Jack. He told my friend he didn't want to be "plugged into the system" and that he *liked* being homeless. As he later wrote, "At the time I initially enjoyed being homeless and the variety of experiences while moving from place to place and spending a lot of time on the streets."

I thought that by refusing to help, by refusing to always bail him out with money or a place to stay that Jack would one day wake up and think: *fuck this for a life!* He would become so fed up with being broke, of begging, hunting for drugs and hanging with all those crazy street people, that he would want to change. But Jack would have to fall further and hurt more before that day would come.

• • •

Jack migrates from his beloved Camden Town and starts hanging out in Lewisham. While begging on the streets he's taken in by a young New-Age hippie couple with two young kids. He goes to live with them in a tent in their garden. Jack says that they were a "sweet" couple who often gave shelter to homeless people and helped them to find inner peace with healthy food, "positive vibes", companionship, spiritual practices (meditation) and sometimes the consumption of organic psychedelics like cacti and mushrooms.

But all their positive vibes and spiritual practices can't get Jack to come out of his self-imposed isolation and connect with this family. He's still recovering from a big acid trip that has left him in full-blown zombie mode; blank mind, dead heart.

These hippie healers really tried to help him. But their love and care was, according to Jack, "all going to waste on someone who was a walking corpse – dead emotionally, dead mentally and who longed to be dead physically."

They wanted Jack to come inside their home and become a part of the family, share supper, play with the kids, talk and confide in the adults. They saw that he needed a place of calm, stability and healing and they were happy to provide this.

But Jack rejected their help; he was too ashamed of the person he'd become to be a part of their family. "I saw myself as a decaying piece of shit. I was an infection in this miniature utopia they were creating in their home. I was convinced that no matter how much I tried to hide the rot, the disease and poison that was at the centre of my existence, they'd be able to sense it."

So instead of trying to integrate with the family, Jack opted for total isolation. He would stay in his tent in the garden for days with no one to talk to and nothing to do. And hungry...so hungry he felt a physical ache. There were times when Jack wouldn't eat all day because to eat meant he would have to go inside their home, sit with the family, make conversation and share their food. But they would see it. See him. See the fucking disease in the room. No. Best stay in the tent and rot.

One time it began to rain hard. The rain seeped into Jack's tent and into his sleeping bag, his clothes and his mind. Jack was cold. Wet. Hungry. Lonely. This was a new level of misery. The two kids were dispatched to try and persuade Jack to come out of the tent and into the house. Dinner was being served.

Jack...Jack...mum says come inside and have food. C'mon Jack! Dinner!

He tells them: No thanks, I'm fine. Not hungry. Cheers.

But they won't give up. It's a game to them, a kid's game called get Jack out of his tent and come have some food. They plead and plead and make promises of delicious things mum has made and Jack lies there and thinks: *Please, just fuck off...leave me alone... leave me to stew in my misery and self-loathing you fucking brats!* Eventually, the kids give up and Jack gets his wish.

After a few weeks, life in the tent proves too much. He's ready to try and change. I'd told him that whenever he was ready to quit taking drugs, get a job and get his life together he could come back and live with me and I would support him for a while. One day I get a text. Can he come and see me? He's ready to change. To quit taking drugs and get his life together. This could be it. The moment when Jack finally gets back on track. My Tough Love policy has finally paid off! Or so I thought.

16

The Rocky Plan

I'd always assumed that at some point Jack's life would change, by accident or design. It would be just another ordinary day in the life of Jack when suddenly something extraordinary would happen; a new thought or a new encounter would change everything. Jack finds God. Jack falls in love. Jack decides he wants to devote his life to working with disabled children or Jack wants to go back into education and get a degree. Jack would come home and he'd be smiling and I'd sense the crackle of his excitement and he'd say, "Guess what happened to me today?" And he'd tell me his exciting news about his new discovery and direction and I would give him a big hug and say: that's so great Jack. I'm so happy for you!

But it never happened.

I couldn't understand how change couldn't change Jack. Change is an inevitable part of life; you can't stop it. But it seemed to me that Jack could. It was as if his inertia made him invincible; time's omnipotent power to generate change was no match for Jack's omnipotent passivity.

And then one day I realised that despite all the help Jack was getting, nothing was really helping him to change and get well. He was plugged into the official network of health care and subjected to mental health evaluations, brain scans, consultations with his GP, various forms of medications and therapists. Plus, he had the unofficial network of a supportive mum and dad and friends.

But it was us – medical professionals, family and friends – who were the main beneficiaries of all this help. It made *us* feel better because a) we were doing our bit, we were caring for Jack and b) it created the comforting illusion that something was being done for Jack. He was getting help and was, presumably, getting better. But Jack didn't feel any better and nothing was changing.

It was around late October 2014 that I decided that something more had to be done about Jack; some form of radical intervention. If Jack couldn't, or wouldn't, save himself, I would have to do it for him. The experts and medical professionals had all tried and failed and now it was up to me. I would give it one last almighty go. I came up with a new idea to try and kick-start a new life for Jack and I called it: The Rocky Plan.

In *Rocky IV*, former heavyweight champion of the world Rocky Balboa (Sylvester Stallone) has given up on boxing and let himself go – but then he decides it's time to change. He undergoes gruelling training sessions in the wilds of Siberia to win the fight against the invincible USSR champion Ivor Drago (Dolph Lundgren). But first he must do battle with himself and rediscover his hunger, his drive, his will; he must find the 'Eye of The Tiger' – remember that song by Survivor? – within.

Ok, Jack wasn't exactly an 'Eye of the Tiger' kind of guy. No, he was more a 'I'm A Loser Baby (So Why Don't You Kill Me)' kind of a guy. I knew my Rocky Plan might seem naïve and simplistic;

a piece of American can-do, self-help silliness. After all, life is not a *Rocky* film and Jack was no Rocky.

But I honestly believed he could be. There are ordinary people – no more capable than Jack – who manage to radically change their lives for the better. People with acute depression and who have attempted suicide (just like Jack), homeless and helpless young men living on the streets (just like Jack), junkies, alcoholics, prostitutes who are able to crawl out of the wreckage of their lives and make a life worth living. So why not Jack? He just needed his dad to give him a helping hand.

I was also fed-up with my sporadic, half-hearted stop-go-stop attempts to help him. It was time to roll up my sleeves and be that dad I said I wanted to be: the dad who does what it takes to save his son's life. I realised that I'd come to accept Jack's depression and suicidal tendencies as normal and worse of all: I'd come to accept there was nothing I could do. How many times had I told myself: *Jack can only change when Jack wants to change!*

Life Lesson Number Ten: *Some People Can't Change Even if They Want to Change*

It seems an obvious truth that people like Jack have to want to change before they can change. But the actual practice of change is more complex than that. Yes, Jack wanted to change but at the same time he didn't want to change. He didn't believe that change was possible and he didn't believe that change could solve his problems. So there was no point in me sitting around twiddling my thumbs waiting for the day that Jack decides he wants to change; he could be dead before then.

Screw that, I thought. And so I came up with my Rocky rescue plan: I would get Jack to agree to a regime of mental and physical exercise to repair that damaged brain of his and get his body into good physical shape. Jack and I would go jogging through the park together; do weights in the gym together, stretch at yoga classes together and sit silently during sessions of mindfulness and meditation together. We'd carefully study the superior self-help books and Jack would abstain from drugs and drink. He would also eat a healthy diet. He'd go back into therapy and keep taking his medication. And he would find a job and keep it. And all the time I would be by his side, cheering him on, pushing him to the limit; pushing him to victory, just like Rocky's trainer. And at the end of it Jack would give me a big hug and say, "thanks Dad. I couldn't have done it without you."

There was just one problem: how in the hell could I get Jack to agree to my Rocky Plan? He hated doing all these sorts of things; to Jack they were all a waste of time. But I knew I could use his death wish to get him to sign on to the Rocky programme. So I offered him this deal: Let me help you get well. Follow my plan for the next six months and I will let you live with me, I will support you financially and if nothing has changed at the end of that time and you still want to die, "we will discuss options."

Of course I was being deliberately vague, so vague that Jack would assume that this meant options as how to die. I had no intention of doing this. My offer was an act of manipulative deception

– a total lie – for which I make no apology. Should he actually complete the six months and he still wanted to die, I could always say that I only said I would *discuss* options – and now that we have discussed options, I'm sorry but my answer is no: I won't help you die.

Jack, foolishly, didn't press me on what I meant by 'options', he was just so thrilled that I might possibly assist his suicide – and he would have a place to stay in the meantime – that he would give it a real go. So I got him to sign a document which basically said, he had to do everything I told him for the next six months and he signed on the dotted line.

• • •

Did I really believe in the Rocky Plan or was that me just indulging in my Super Dad fantasy so that I could feel good about myself? Maybe. But I honestly thought that if I could get Jack to follow the Rocky Plan it would definitely help him. I knew that my methods were sound, but I wasn't sure about Jack's motives. Even though he claimed he sincerely wanted to give my plan a go, I had doubts. Was he just playing me along so I would financially support him and he would have a place to live? Was I his saviour or his sucker? Could he last the course and could I last Jack for six months?

I decided that I had to stay positive and focused on trying to help him. I had to keep smiling. I had to keep telling Jack – and myself – that *we're going to beat this thing!* I had to be that dad: The Good Dad. His Rocky Moment was my Rocky Moment too. I had to step up to the plate, reach inward and find the inner resources to help me save Jack's life.

The following are extracts from a diary I kept during the Rocky period.

Rocky Plan: Day One

8a.m. I bring Jack a cup of tea in bed. He's fast asleep. His laptop is by his side, like the comfort toy a child always goes to sleep with. I'm wearing a tracksuit. I have bought a whistle and I have a clipboard with a sheet of paper on it that is headed, Rocky Plan: Day One. (Give a dad a whistle and clipboard and he becomes a new man.) I've already been for a run, showered, shaved and I give my new whistle a loud blow and cry, "Rise and shine Rocky!"

Jack doesn't stir. He groans and pleads for a lay in: "Dad, I didn't get much sleep last night." He begs for extra time in bed.

I say he can stay in bed while I cook breakfast.

"But I'm not hungry"

"Nonsense! You need a big healthy breakfast to begin the first day of the rest of your new life!"

Jack dives back under the duvet and groans.

"You're mine, bitch!" I say, waving a copy of our contract at him.

After breakfast I make a plan for Jack's day. Item One: Change Jack's appearance. He needs a new look to help him make a new life. The fact that he agrees to let me cut his dreads off is a good sign. I try to cut them with scissors but they are rock hard; it's like he's been using superglue as a hair conditioner. I try a large sharp carving knife. No luck. I go and get a saw and give my son a haircut. Jack looks at himself in the mirror and says: "Man what have you done to me? I look so weird!" He does look a little weird because some of the dreads just won't come off. Oh, well.

Later, I gave him money to buy some new trainers, new jeans and new T-shirts. When I came back home I found a transformed Jack. He'd shaved and he looked clean and handsome. What a great start! "You're a good-looking young man!" I said. "Together, we're going to beat this thing, right?"

"Yeah, I guess so," says Jack.

"No, sorry. No guess-so-shit. We're gonna to do it – or die trying!"

Jack grins at me and says, "Can't we just do the die bit without the try bit? Only kidding dad."

Although Jack thanked me for the money, I could tell the change in his appearance made no difference to him. I told myself that's ok, it would take time. I have to learn to be patient, just as Jack has to learn to be positive.

Then I got him to do about ten minutes of exercise – mostly stretching out on the terrace. I tell him about the importance of breathing deeply as a way of keeping calm and focused. "Breathing can help you find inner freedom."

Jack laughs and says, "Dad, do you really believe that shit?"

"No negativity, thank you!" I reply "Breathe in…1-2-3…breath out. Annnnnd…stretch!"

Jack breathes. Jack Stretches. Jack is getting with the programme!

I'm feeling very optimistic.

And then we had a row.

I noticed that one of the laces of his new trainers had come undone. When I pointed this out to him, Jack said it didn't matter. Here's what followed.

Me: Yes, it does matter. Would you please tie it up?

Jack: Why? What difference does it make?

Me: Because, it's about you caring about your appearance.

Jack: I don't care about my appearance – you do.

Me: But it's all a part of your rehabilitation and creating a new Jack.

Jack: Wot? Save a life through a shoelace? Man, that's so fucking insane, even for you!

Me: Jack, taking pride in the way you look is important. It also influences the way people perceive and treat you.

Jack: But you always told me I shouldn't care what other people say about the way you look and think. You said that you should live your life the way you want to.

Me: Well fuck that for the moment. Please, just tie your shoe-laces. We have an agreement. I wave his signed copy in the air.

He leans down to tie his lace.

Jack: Man, I don't like being treated like a slave.

Watching Jack reluctantly tie his shoelace I realise that it's only day one and I've already turned into a cross between Nurse Ratched from *One Flew Over the Cuckoo's Nest* and the drill sergeant from *Full Metal Jacket*. Why did tying the shoe lace matter so much to me? Because his reluctance to do it was symptomatic of his whole why bother?/can't be arsed attitude to life. In this small detail I saw the bigger drama of Jack's retreat from life. The lace undone was the life left undone.

But for Jack not wanting to tie the lace was an assertion of his autonomy, and that despite the Rocky contract he still had some small control of his life.

Later that day I came back from shopping. "I got just what you need!"

"What's that", asks Jack, "Drugs? A gun to shoot myself with? Yeah dad, I know: no negativity."

"Here you go all the tools necessary for change!" and I empty the bag on the kitchen table. There are diaries, notebooks – moleskine and lined ones – life planners, year planners, yellow stickers, blue sticky notes, thumb tacks, packets of pencils, multi-coloured highlighters, a pencil sharpener, a rubber and a box of Bic biros.

I try and explain to Jack my philosophy of stationery. "I've always found that in a time of crisis the most effective course of action for getting your life sorted is to go for a big stationary shop. Look at all these beauties!"

But Jack does not see the beauty of new stationery and its implicit promise of a new beginning; he just looks at me like I'm crazy and comes and gives me a small pat on the back and says, "Cheers, dad. Keep taking your medication."

I ask him to write down an account of what he is going through. He responds with the usual: what's-the-point?/waste-of-time/why-bother?/who-gives-a-fuck? I calmly point out that it will help me to understand his situation. He actually writes a long account which I plan to read later.

Rocky Plan: Day Two

At breakfast we draw up a list of things for Jack to do: clean kitchen floor, do some cooking, do some charity work, wash sheets and air out his mattress. Amazingly, he's does most of them! In the afternoon we do a session of meditation together. I put on a YouTube 'Ten Minute Mind-Calming Meditation' video, complete with Tibetan bells and chants. I get Jack to cross his legs and we followed the instructions for deep breathing. And then we began to chant, "omm…ommm…ommm."

Jack shakes his head and said, this is so fucked-up!

I said, just give it a try, will you.

He did and for the next ten minutes Jack actually sat still and got into it. At the end of our session he tells me, "yeah, that was pretty cool."

Rocky Plan: Day Five

Jack refuses to go jogging or go to the gym. He doesn't want to learn how to cook. I could evoke our contract but I let it go. I suggest he might try and do something creative with all that pain and depression of his. We have the following exchange.

Me: Why not keep a diary-journal? It could become a classic account of what it's like to be someone in your position. Depression stuff really sells. Did you ever read *Prozac Nation*? You're a really good writer. What do you say?

Jack: Naaah.

Me: Ok. Maybe write a film about what you're going through? You used to be really into films. Make it into a psychological horror film – you know depression as this demon entering the minds of youth. Ok, that's lame so give it your own twist.

Jack: Naaah.

Me: Couldn't you at least write a classic rock song of depression and angst? You're into all that Nine Inch Nails, I-wanna-die stuff.

Jack: Dad, that's such a cliché!

Me: Can't you do something?

Jack: How about I top myself?

Me: Go ahead. Knock yourself out.

Jack: (laughing) I keep trying!

We have both violated the no-negativity rule of our agreement.

Rocky Plan: Day Six

Today I made real progress! Not with Jack but with me. We had the following conversation. Jack said: "You don't understand. Everyone is worthless to me. People around me are like dead people. I feel nothing for them." Normally I would have felt hurt and angry by this and retaliated with something nasty like, *Ok, if that's the case, then just fuck off!* But I don't. I stay calm and say, "Yes, but we dead, worthless people love you."

"Yeah, whatever," says Jack.

Rocky Plan: Day Seven

Jack comes back from his second therapy session. How did it go I ask?

Complete waste of time, he tells me.

With Jack, everything is a waste of time.

I suggest he try working at a local charity shop? It would help him ease back into working full time.

Complete waste of time, he says.

I asked if he read that book I bought him on *The Science of Positive Thinking?*

Complete waste of time, said Jack.

For a man who spends his time wasting time, it's odd that he condemns things as a waste of time. It's as if these wastes of time will interfere with his time wasting.

I ask him, "Is what we're doing a waste of time?"

Jack says, "Nah. I really appreciate what you're doing. I want to give it a go."

He knows that's what I want to hear, but I suspect he doesn't believe it.

Rocky Plan: Day Nine

Jack is acting strange. Kind of hyper. He goes around doing his brain song. "My brain, my brain – who will stop the pain of my damaged brain?"

He is back to talking about a very different form of self-help: suicide. He tells me that while I was out of the flat he tried to kill himself with a belt around his neck, but he couldn't make it work. But he's not downhearted, because he wasn't scared, and he found that counting helped him to stay calm. If that's the case, why the hell should I bother trying to help? I might as well give up right now.

Rocky Plan: Day Ten

We have a terrible row about £20 that I lent him which he swore he would pay back and doesn't. (It's not about the money, it's about taking responsibility.) I suddenly lose all hope of change and say despairingly that this isn't going to work. Jack stays silent.

Rocky Plan: Day Twelve

I went into the front room this morning and was confronted by Jack's pong. He lay there asleep surrounded by the usual Jack's detritus: I could see traces of tobacco on the floor and a red rizla packet by the lamp, a sign that he has been getting stoned. Use of drugs is an immediate deal breaker.

Rocky Plan: Day Fifteen

I have just been talking to Jack and decided to quit. He was telling me how he appreciated what I was doing but change was impossible. It was too late for a recovery. And even if by some miracle he did recover, it was only a matter of time before he relapsed back into his present state.

Suddenly, a wave of exhaustion came over me. I knew that I could never get through to him. It was as if he did not want to leave the comfort of his discomfort; he was clinging to his illness.

What could I do? His despair had finally defeated my hope. I have to accept that Jack is right: he's fucked. I tell him that I quit – at this he panics and he says that he would like to keep going but I know he's just saying that so I won't kick him out. Operation Rocky is over.

One last thing, I say.

What?

"Don't commit suicide in my flat. You hear me? I don't want to come home and find you hanging from a rope and freaking me out."

"No way," said Jack, "I plan to go with pills."

• • •

I was disappointed that my Rocky rescue plan had ended in failure. And now looking back I'm disappointed that I gave up so easily. Wouldn't a stronger dad have just carried on and on and never given up? We had both failed the Rocky Test.

It was only after his death that I read the statement he wrote about what was going on in his head during that time and I realised that I didn't stand a chance. Jack was too far gone and he was just playing me along.

Here is an extract of what Jack wrote:

I believe that I'm beyond the point of getting better largely due to the fact that I lost the essence of myself in 2012. Each time I've 'got better,' I've returned to a life that was increasingly hollow, dysfunctional and unsatisfying on every level, hence the constant drug use and ever-increasing desperate measures to procure drugs, such as begging, and the constant edging towards violence, death and criminality. I know in my heart that my life is over and nothing will ever convince me otherwise… All I want now is a peaceful and certain death free of the terror, pain and suffering I've endured for most of my life and I think I have earned that right. I've suffered an incredible amount and continue to do so, no aspect of life interests me anymore… I no longer have any interest in getting better.

So the whole thing had just been a con. Jack had been conning me so as to have a place to live and financial support until he could die – and I had been conning myself, to think I really was the Good Dad who could save his son.

17

Christmas Without You

2015

This is my first Christmas without you. And from now on every Christmas will have you and your suicide lurking in the shadows of the festive fun. You are the dead son people are careful not to mention while exchanging presents or family anecdotes. You are the dead son I didn't want to remember or talk about – at least not on Christmas day. I don't want kids to see me and wonder why the old guy in front of the TV with the glass of Baileys and the Christmas edition of the *Radio Times* looks so sad. I don't want Dexter to start asking at regular intervals, "Dad, are you ok?"

But Christmas without you is not an option; there are no distractions powerful enough to drown you out for the day. You are now my very own Ghost of Christmas Past. You came to me that day creeping through my mind, all pale and putrid, opening old wounds like they were Christmas presents. I keep leaving the room to cry.

Thanks Jack.

And merry fucking Christmas.

• • •

This Christmas I wanted to get away from my flat and myself and all those memories of you – The Other Jack – spending Christmas with me. So I go to stay with Maxine and Dexter (and Maxine's boyfriend Ian) in Grantham. We have a huge tree that looks like an overdressed drag queen, floating on a silvery sea of beautifully wrapped presents. It's a proper Christmas, not like those token affairs you and I had with the six-inch tree bearing one bauble and those Bernard Matthews turkey slices you loved. (I will never understand how you liked that shit more than a proper oven cooked turkey.) Anyway, everyone is having a brilliant time. I'm having a wonderful time too – and then you come to visit me.

I was watching Dexter by the tree and he was lost in a frenzy of present opening; ripping off the wrapping paper, getting to the treasure inside, then discarding it and grabbing another present. And doing it again. And again. Dexter was high and happy on a present binge. I looked at his happiness and I wondered: were you ever this happy at Christmas? You must have been, at least when you were his age.

Everyone assumed that Christmas this year would be hard for me: it being my first Christmas without you. But you and I know that we didn't really enjoy spending Christmas together: we hated it. When my parents were alive we'd go to their house on Christmas day, that was fun, wasn't it? I could never tell with you. You hid your true feelings behind an impenetrable façade of politeness. Had you reached that point where nothing – nothing but getting wrecked – was fun? But when they died it was Christmas for two: just you and me.

I remember one Christmas us sitting at my kitchen table, you at one end and me at the other, wearing our paper Christmas hats.

You didn't like real turkey and I refused to get you those Bernard Matthews turkey slices, so we had chicken instead. The chicken was dry and the roast potatoes weren't crunchy. The sprouts were hard and the gravy was too watery. I had so wanted to make you a nice Christmas meal and failed.

I said to you, "This is the most depressing dinner I've ever cooked in my life. Sorry."

You said, "No man, it's good!"

The funny thing is, you weren't trying to cheer me up or be polite; you really enjoyed that terrible meal and that made it all the more depressing!

As usual when we ate together, we struggled to make conversation and took turns to ask each other questions.

So, how's it going?

What you been up to?

How's x?

Seen any movies?

How's the writing going?

What are you listening to?

And blah, blah, blah.

Why was it so hard for us to talk? The funny thing is that I could talk to anyone – anyone but you. We had nothing to talk about, except your depression. (And not even you wanted to talk about that at the Christmas dinner table.) That's what made me so sad. We just had. . . nothing to say to each other. And I don't mean confessional, daddy-son-I-love-you shit. And I don't mean Big Existential, What's-It-All-About-Alfie? stuff either. I mean ordinary, silly-everyday-things. Gossip. Family stories. Funny anecdotes. Just stuff to share. I've seen other dads do it with their sons, why not us?

And the terrible irony is: I have so much I could talk to you about now.

I guess the conditions weren't right for funny repartee or conversation. After all, you were depressed and I was depressed. We were two lonely, depressed people eating over-cooked chicken on Christmas day in silence. These Christmas Q&A sessions were good for about fifteen minutes and then our attempt at conversation would fade out, and we'd sit in silence.

And you'd say, "Shall we watch a movie?"

And I said, "Yeah, let's do that."

A movie together, that would be fun! We'll have ice cream together and watch a film like people do on a Christmas afternoon. Brill!

But then we couldn't find a movie we both wanted to watch. I wanted to watch Christmassy movies like *Oliver*. *It's A Wonderful Life*. *Scrooge*.

You wanted to watch *Scarface, Natural Born Killers, the Texas Chainsaw Massacre*.

I said: "I'm not watching *The Texas Chainsaw Massacre* during Christmas dinner!"

And you said: "Why not? It's a classic!"

"For heaven's sake Jack! *Oliver* is a Christmas classic not the bloody *Texas Chainsaw Massacre!*"

"So?"

I couldn't be bothered to explain it to you, so I just gave up and let you choose. I figured the buzz of Leather Face's chainsaw was better than the sound of silence. But it wasn't long before I drifted off to the sitting room and left you alone at the table.

• • •

I keep thinking: what if instead of being dead you'd been there with me in Grantham for Christmas? I know what would have happened. Maxine – and her brother Martin – would have made sure you got lots of presents: socks you hated. DVDs of films you wouldn't want to watch. Aftershave you would never use and some silly, novelty items from Dexter. And you would have said: "Cheers! Wicked! Thanks!" and, "That's so kind of you!" – and you would have meant it too. But you'd have felt bad that you hadn't bought any gifts for these kind people. You would have hung around the sidelines of the sitting room with the laptop on your knees, and every so often you'd look up and say to Max or me, "Is there anything I can do to help?"

But then sensing that dinner was almost ready you would have snuck off to your room. You would have been terrified to sit at the dinner table with all those good, kind people that you couldn't talk to. You would want to spare them – and yourself – the embarrassment, the social agony of having you – Jack the Zombie – at the table.

Maxine would ask me, "Cos, call Jack for dinner."

I would call out your name a few times and then go up to your room. And there I'd find you in bed, plugged into your laptop. At first you'd say you weren't hungry or you weren't feeling well. And when that didn't work, you'd say what you always said: *I can't be with people. All that kindness makes it worse…makes me feel like shit. I should feel something, but I don't feel anything. I can't give anything back. It's agony. I feel such a useless dumb-ass. I can't go back down there. Please dad, let me stay here.*

And instead of staying calm and talking you through your anxiety, I'd get angry and say: for fuck's sake Jack! Could you just cool it with the I-can't-feel-anything routine for one fucking day? Just take a deep breath and lighten up! Come down stairs. Have a few drinks and enjoy yourself. Please! Just do it for me. Just for one day – be fucking normal!

And then it would be your turn to get angry: *No man you don't understand. I'm fuckin' in hell! HELL! I can't be around people. It's torture! Why can't you understand that? Why can't you try and help me instead of making me feel worse? I can't do this. I can't go on like this. I'm going to top myself!*

And I'd make some cruel crack like, "Really? I should have got you some rope for Christmas instead of socks."

Here's a funny thing that you'll like. The next day we were all meant to go to Maxine's brother's house for a Boxing Day lunch. But I couldn't face it. I wanted to stay in bed. She pleaded with me to come, saying it would cheer me up. But I did a Jack and said no I can't…sorry I just can't face them. I can't be with people. I was so sad about you that I had to stay in bed. And so that was my first Christmas without you.

Oh, I forgot to mention that Max gave me two wonderful presents: a pair of socks and the number of a good therapist.

18

Lost Connections

After the failure of Operation Rocky, Jack and I row and he leaves my place. Once again I tell myself: I have to let Jack go and let him sort out his own life. He's twenty-seven-years-old for heaven's sakes! There's nothing more I can do. I know his mum feels the same way.

Jack hits the streets of Camden Town and falls in with his old druggy crowd. He sells weed, smokes weed, shoplifts – and always gets caught. He goes to live with a bunch of anarchist squatters in Hoxton – but Jack pisses-off everyone there and they kick him out. He sofa surfs until he runs out of sofas. He turns to an old friend of mine Michelle for help and a place to stay. But when she tries to encourage him to take a bit of responsibility for finding a place – i.e., fill out a couple of forms – Jack turns on her, accusing her of being another "shithead who had let him down". She puts the phone down on him.

Something is happening to Jack: Sweet Jack is giving way to angry Jack. Sooner or later Jack falls out with everyone: family, friends, people who try and help him, people who love him. He even falls out with his druggy street crowd – "fucking scum" he calls them.

As Jack's anger and isolation grows and festers, it expresses itself in outbursts of Travis Bickle (Bickle was the alienated urban loner of Martin Scorsese's *Taxi Driver*) like rants that Jack spews out on his Facebook page. He likes quoting Bickle's famous *Taxi Driver* prophecy that, "someday a real rain will come and wash all the scum off the streets." On Facebook Jack rants against "degenerate scum" and "filthy white-trash chav cunts" who should be "euthanized for the fucking sake of humanity."

And he's getting into fights. In Jack's version he's always the innocent victim of some complete "cunt" who pours beer on him, gives him a push or starts picking on him for no reason. Jack denies he's ever provocative or to blame. He doesn't get it. Jack calls himself the "most chilled-out person in Camden." So why, he wonders, "does this shit happen to me?"

Sometimes during those crazy Camden Town nights, things turn nasty. On New Year's eve at a club called The Slimelight Jack gets into trouble. "Some bloke tried showing me up in front of his lady friends, with disastrous results for him." (He doesn't say what that was, but I suspect it ended in violence.) Another time Jack is at a friend's birthday party and throws a pint of beer at a bouncer. Jack gets thrown out. He sneaks back in and gets thrown out again. He gets thrown out of clubs and pubs and he's banned from supermarkets (for shoplifting) and gets into angry confrontations with staff at banks and shops.

When I once asked Jack why he was always getting into fights and having all these angry confrontations he told me, "It's because I won't put up with people's shit. I won't be disrespected."

Jack was making a stand. For him it was a matter of principle, his one-man protest. It was as if he'd lost everything in life, but a little bit of dignity. He demanded nothing from this shit world but a modicum of respect. He had to have a little bit of respect from the world because he had none for himself.

I always thought that part of Jack's problem in getting his life together was that he was Jack. He was lazy, undisciplined, irresponsible – a silly middle-class boy seduced by the sleazy romance of street life. In that world he didn't have to grow-up and give up his adolescent pleasures and pursuits. He was homeless, unemployed and broke because he had made a foolish and self-destructive lifestyle choice.

His mum and I tried to warn him about how if he didn't change he would end up homeless – or worse: dead before he was thirty. (That was Julie's prophecy sent to me in an email.) But Jack ignored us and ignored everyone including his buddy Jake. One evening they were watching *Killing Zoe* – one of Jack's favourite films – and Jake was telling Jack that he needed to get a job and get his shit together. "I was trying to help him. But helping Jack was so frustrating! I always felt like I was banging my head against a wall." "You're just making me feel worse", Jack said.

Why did a smart boy like Jack make so many bad choices? Why couldn't he break the cycle of homelessness-drugs-unemployment and try and make a better life for himself? Yes, he was partly driven by mindless, adolescent hedonism but he was also driven by a deep self-hatred. I knew he suffered from low self-esteem but I never appreciated the intensity of his self-loathing. I found a psychological worksheet that Jack had filled out for one of his therapists. Under the heading of "Self-critical Thoughts" – where you were meant to list all the critical thoughts you had of yourself – Jack has written: *cunt, bastard, brain-damaged freak, piece of shit, tramp, grotesque, Mr. Disgusting, smelly cunt, fat disgusting cunt* and: *I've ruined my relationships.*

No one was as disappointed and disgusted by Jack as Jack was. It was what made change so urgent and at the same time so impossible. If like Jack, you're convinced that this is who you are, then it's hard to imagine a happy future for yourself – a future with a wife, a job, and maybe a kid – for one simple reason: shit like you doesn't deserve a future. You have no right to happiness and you have no means to happiness.

• • •

Even when he wasn't angry and getting into fights or stoned and acting like a goofball, Jack could still alienate people. Jake told me, "Jack had a knack for rubbing people up the wrong way. It got worse as he got older."

Jack would be hanging out with people and someone would start going on about some band they love and how *fucking awesome* they are and everyone would agree. But not Jack. He won't stay silent and obey the social rule that says: *thou shall not slag-off someone's favourite band!* Especially a band they love; a band who defines who they are.

And so, out it pops from Jack's mouth: *Man, that band are such fucking shit! I can't believe you like them!* And he might give a snort of derision and shake his head in disbelief that you could actually be such a dumb ass to love a band as crappy as that band! *Dude, what is wrong with you!*

That's so rude of him! That's so disrespectful! If you say to someone that their beloved band is shit, you're in effect saying that person is shit too.

But Jack didn't care. I don't think he was deliberately setting out to offend; Jack wasn't a wind-up merchant who enjoyed being provocative and causing trouble for the sake of it. He was usually very polite. But Jack had his opinion and you were going to hear his opinion whether you liked it or not. Is it a coincidence that his mum made her name in journalism, writing for the *NME* in the 1970s by slagging off people's favourite bands too?

Consequently, Jake always felt nervous about introducing Jack to his other mates because he knew this would happen. At some point in the evening Jack would cause trouble by simply being Jack. Jake tried to tell Jack to stop pissing people off. "You don't make it easy for yourself do you?" Jake said.

"Fuck them," said Jack, "I'll say what I want."

When Jake told me this story – a year after Jack's death – I felt that little tingle of parental pride I'd always longed for. I love the way Jack stood up for the things – bands, opinions or people – he believed in. For an anxious, timid and shy boy he could at times be brave.

• • •

During this time I didn't see much of Jack. We'd had another bust-up and Jack had sent me a threatening email that really upset me. After a passage of not speaking to Jack, Tessa – a friend who was looking after him – sent me an email saying Jack was in a bad way and it would be good if I could arrange to see him. I arranged to meet in a café near Tessa's place. As soon as I entered I saw Jack sitting there in his dirty hoody and his usual scruffy self seemed to have an extra layer of grunge.

And then I saw that he had a black eye.

He told me he'd been beaten up. I don't remember if it was over a drug deal or just a fight. I just know that I felt this primal wave of anger and love. I wanted to protect him. I wanted to get the guys who did this to him and do them harm. It was like he was my bullied young boy back at school all over again.

We have tea and he tells me he wants to get his life together – find a job, quit drugs, get away from street life. Of course I've heard this one before, but he sounds sincere so I write to his mum saying I've seen Jack and we need to do something. We agree to pay a deposit for a room that Jack has found in a house in Harrow. Jack is happy. He sends me an email thanking me for my help. He tells me, "I really think things are going to pan out differently this time. I want to get my life back on track – you were right about that drug shit."

He's never said that before and now I'm wondering if this is the turning point in Jack's life.

In A White Room

I picture Jack in his white cube of a room in Harrow. It smells of old pizza boxes and Jack pong. Maybe he's high, maybe he's low. It's early evening or late at night and Jack is hunched over his laptop, posting messages on Facebook. He is like a shipwrecked sailor stranded on a desert island sending out distress signals, calling out into the cyber darkness requests for rescue.

"Anyone down to party tonight?" (March 11, 2015)

No one responds.

"Anyone fancy having me over to crash for a few nights to a week from Monday?" (March 19, 2015)

No one responds.

"Where da party at?" (March 21, 2015)

No one responds.

"Anyone want to play in Shoreditch tonight?" (March 26, 2015)

No one responds.

"It's so lonely when you don't even know yourself" (20th January 2015)

No one responds.

Jack had over 200 Facebook friends.

• • •

That little white room was meant to free Jack from all the horrors of homelessness and give him a stable base upon which he could build his new life. It freed him from the streets only to isolate him in suburbia. Unable to create a new life, Jack was left in a life even more lonely.

Me: Jack, why didn't you ever call me when you were feeling lonely?

Jack: I did, once! You were with Alice at the cinema. I asked if you could come back to the flat and maybe we could hang out and watch a movie together. I was feeling so down, so lonely.

Me: And what did I say?

Jack: You laughed and said something sarcastic like: oh boy, that will be fun! Saturday night with old laughing-boy Jack! I guess I'll just rush right over!

Me: Fuck! What a dickhead I was. Sorry.

Jack: No biggie. Still, you did come over the next day and we hung out together.

Me: That doesn't excuse me. I should have been there when you needed me. Some dad, eh?

Jack: Dad, are you going to beat yourself up for the rest of your life about this?

Me: Probably.

Jack: Ok. Enjoy!

Jack hated that room in Harrow. He was always trying to think of excuses why he could come and stay with me for the night: he'd say he had an early doctor's appointment/an early interview for a job or had to sign-on really early. Sometimes I said yes, sometimes no.

Jack never wanted a place of his own; his own Jack room. Back in 2012 his mother had rented him a nice room in Brighton – but Jack never moved in. Jack didn't want his own space, he wanted a home. A place that was safe and with a caring parent to watch over him.

The Jack Shower

It soon became clear to me that Jack wasn't changing at all. He was back taking drugs and just drifting along. His dependency on me was not diminishing and my resentment was growing and lead to the Great Shower Row.

One day in 2015 Jack came over to my place and said, "Dad is it ok if I take a shower?"

"No!" I said.

"Why not?" he asked.

"Because you could have taken a shower at your place."

"I didn't think of that."

"No you bloody well didn't!"

"I will next time…so can I take a shower now."

"No!" I shouted and let rip with a Job-like wail of frustration, as if I'd been pushed beyond human endurance by my son's unreasonable request to take a shower.

I know what you're thinking: why didn't I just let him have a shower? What's the big deal? How does it hurt you? It's just a shower. Oh no, that's where you're wrong. Reader, it's not just a shower. It's a Jack shower.

And a Jack shower is never a simple, straightforward thing that can be granted without a second thought. You can't just say sure, have a shower and carry on doing whatever you're doing before and after the Jack shower; you have to take part in the whole Jack shower process. A Jack shower requires strategic planning and personal participation; it involves your time and thought and decisions and revisions. It eats into your time, disrupts your life and alters your mood.

And the Jack request for a shower usually came when I was busy trying to write. I want to carry on writing but I can't, because Jack wants to take a shower. And that means there are all sorts of issues that have to be addressed and resolved before Jack can have his shower and I can get back to writing.

JACK SHOWER ISSUE ONE: CHOOSING A TOWEL FOR JACK

Jack will come, knock on my office door and ask me: "Dad, sorry to bother you, but which towel should I use?"

It's a good question – one that raises important issues about personal hygiene, parental responsibility, individual autonomy – and why I have become such a prissy bourgeois dick who actually cares about which towel his son uses? But I do.

So I leave my desk to go and find Jack a clean towel. I suspect that Jack wouldn't mind if the towel wasn't that clean, which makes me wonder: why bother looking for a clean towel for Jack? As long as it's not covered in excrement, Jack won't notice. I could give him one of the funky towels I've been meaning to wash and he wouldn't mind. He doesn't care about stuff like clean towels, clean sheets, clean sinks and clean bathrooms.

But I do. I could not in good conscience give him an unclean towel. What kind of shitty dad does that? The question for me is: how *clean*, how *good* a towel do I give Jack? So I have to go and find an appropriate towel for Jack. I don't want to give him one of my special A-List towels I keep in reserve for female guests to use the next morning – and I don't want to give him a towel from the dirty laundry basket. So I've got to leave my desk and search and sniff out a towel for Jack's shower. "Hold on" I say. "I'll get you one."

JACK SHOWER STEP TWO: CHECK SHAMPOO

I also have to make sure there's shampoo in the shower. If there's no shampoo left, Jack might not wash his hair. (He thinks if you give it a good soaking that's enough.) I want him to wash his hair and wash away the grime and the grease of that long, tramp hair of his.

I want him to wash away the grime and the grease of that tramp life of his. I want him to step out of that shower all clean and shining with hope and smelling of a fresh start.

"Here's some new shampoo I got for you," I say.

"Cheers."

I go back to my desk. Back to my work. But I don't work. I sit and wait for the next step in the Jack shower process.

JACK SHOWER STEP THREE: ONCE THE TOWEL HAS BEEN USED – WHAT THEN?

After he has finished his shower, Jack will come and knock on my office door and ask me: "sorry to bother you but where should I put this towel?" and I will think: exactly in the same place where I told you to put it last time you asked! But I don't say it because he won't remember where that was. I will tell him: "put it on the radiator".

And he will do this, but he won't spread out the towel properly so it can dry.

So I get up from my desk and I take the towel from him and say, "let me take care of that."

"Cheers," he says.

JACK SHOWER STEP FOUR: THE STATE OF THE BATHROOM POST JACK SHOWER

From my desk I will ask Jack if he's cleaned the bath (it's a bathtub with a shower in it) and he will insist that he has. "Fine" I say and I try and get on with my work but I will keep thinking about the bathtub – the dirt, the hair, the water that has not gone all the way down the plug hole and will leave a limescale stain. And then there's the bathroom floor which Jack will not have wiped properly.

So I get up from my desk, I sigh, and go off to clean up the bathroom, after Jack.

JACK SHOWER STEP FIVE: A SAD SIGHTING OF JACK

Post-shower, Jack will walk around my flat with long wet hair and a towel around his waist and he will search through his black dustbin bags for some clean clothes. And I will see his skinny, pale body and those self-harm scars that stretch and crisscross along his arms and it will make me sad.

JACK SHOWER STEP SIX: CAN I BORROW? Part One

I will go back to my room and instead of writing I will think about Jack and his scars. And Jack will come knock on my office door and say, "sorry to bother you, but do you have any clean socks I can borrow?"

I could just say go to my sock drawer and help yourself. But because I don't want him to take my good socks I get up and go get Jack some socks. I give Jack a pair of clean socks.

JACK SHOWER STEP SEVEN: CAN I BORROW? Part Two

Five minutes later there's a knock at my door: "Sorry to bother you, but do you have a T-shirt I could borrow?"

And I will get up from my desk and go find a T-shirt. Jack will accompany me to veto certain T-shirts on the grounds of taste. He will reject the first four or five T-shirts of mine on the grounds they'll make him look like a 'dick'. I'm tempted to say beggars can't be choosers – but Jack is actually doing a lot of begging on the streets and I don't want to be called an 'insensitive cunt' by Jack.

JACK'S SHOWER STEP EIGHT:

Back at my desk I should be thinking about whatever I'm currently writing. But I can't because I'm thinking about Jack and the fact that come tomorrow – or the day after – we will go through the whole Jack shower routine again. And do you know what really bugs me about the whole Jack shower scenario? Jack can take a shower and change his clothes and never look any cleaner. Nothing changes for Jack, but his socks.

So on that day when I shouted at him about taking a shower, Jack gave me the *dad-you're-being-crazy* look and says: "Man, it's just a shower!"

"No Jack. It's a Jack shower!"

How did Jack feel about me saying no to his shower request and shouting at him? Shortly after the no shower incident Jack wrote an email to me that read:

You know I have a seriously unpleasant life which I'm planning to bring to a close soon. I would've thought it would make you happy to make things a bit easier for me by allowing me to take a shower and contact my friends when I have no other means of doing so, instead it makes you angry and unhappy – that's not healthy. Most family members and friends would just be like 'yea cool, go for it.'

Later we talked about it and he said to me that what really upset him was the way I said no; my irritation, my anger.

Jack said to me, "Couldn't you try and say no with a bit of kindness?"

Of course he was right: see Life Lesson Number One: *Be kind*.

• • •

I resented Jack's shower request because I resented Jack. I resented his dependency; his whole incompetent-incapable-disabling fucked-up-stoner-immaturity. I was annoyed by Jack and his end-less requests:

Dad, can I take a shower?

Dad, can I borrow £20?

Dad, can I borrow your phone?

Dad, can I borrow your computer?

Dad, can I take that bottle of wine with me?

Dad, can I borrow some socks?

Dad, can I crash here tonight?

Dad, can I get a stamp from you?

Dad, can I make a cup of tea?

Dad, can I make a cup of coffee?

Dad, can I use your Oyster card?

Dad, can I put some things in the wash?

Dad, can I use your razor?

Dad, can I turn on the heating?

Dad, can you pay my rent?

Dad, can you get me some new trainers?

I had to say no to the shower, didn't I? I had to draw a line in the sand and create boundaries, establish rules and set out expectations. I had to say to my son: enough! In saying yes to the shower I was saying yes to a life of dependency on me and everyone who knew Jack. I wanted Jack to try to take a bit of responsibility for his life. Was I the Bad Dad of the Century for wanting my twenty-eight-year-old son to grow-up and be responsible?

And now I wish to God I had let him take that shower – or at least had said no in a kinder way.

19

Where's Jack?

Death stinks. If you haven't discovered the dead body of your loved one, death will help you find it; just follow your nose. The stink of putrefaction is death's way of saying: *Yoo-hoo! Over here! In here! Behind this door/in this closet/in this bed/in this room…*

Sunday 28th June 2015. Around 5pm Jack's housemates have got together because of the smell. They've noticed it for the past two or three days. That funny odour has turned bad and now it's a full-on stink that can't be ignored or dismissed as a blocked drain. At first they thought it was coming from the toilet, but on that Sunday the four housemates searched for the smell.

They had one clue: the smell was worst near Jack's room.

So they knocked on his door. No answer. They listened for the sounds of Jack and heard silence. They gave the door a push. It opened a little bit – just a few inches – but something inside was stopping them from opening it all the way. From the door's small gap came a blast of stink as strong as a wave of heat from a furnace. No doubt about it, the smell was coming from Jack's room.

But where was Jack?

One of the housemates took a peek through the gap of the door and thought he saw blood on the floor. He put his phone around the door and took three photos to see if Jack was inside; in one of them they could see a pair of legs on the floor. Someone has another go at pushing the door open – it opens just enough to take a proper look inside and there's Jack's slumped body.

They called for an ambulance. Shortly after the ambulance arrived two police officers turned up. The police push the door open and enter Jack's room. It's dark. The window blind is down and the smell is so terrible that one of the police officers raised the blind and opened the window.

Here's what the police found in Jack's room: old pizza boxes, a pool of blood on the floor, his laptop, a DVD player, clothes, books, a crack pipe, a printout from the internet on how to kill yourself. And they found a printout of an email from his mum that reads:

"You're VERY CLEVER and you have to stop looking on the dark side. Volunteer for a charity and you'll meet people that way. Go back to university! My friend got her degree at FIFTY!

In Israel now, I'll take you out in London next month?

ALWAYS

Your Mum, Who Loves you"

• • •

The police found Jack, behind the door in a sitting position with his head hanging down. He had a white towel wrapped around his neck and a black cord around that; the chord was tied to the silver door hook at the top of the door.

There are basically two types of death by hanging. One is the drop hanging that is used in public executions and often features in Hollywood films or television dramas. A trap door is opened beneath the feet of the condemned man, they fall, they swing, squirm and die.

This rarely happens when it comes to hanging by suicide. The more common form is what is known as the 'suspension hanging' – or 'partial hanging'. Here the toes or feet will be touching the ground and the body can be sitting or kneeling down. The noose is tightened around the neck by a person's own bodyweight and it cuts off the supply of oxygen to the lungs and blood to the brain which causes asphyxiation and death. This is how Jack died.

How did he look slumped against that door with his self made noose around his neck? PC Harpreet Kaur Sidhu of the Harrow police describes Jack like this: "There laid an apparent lifeless body of a white male with long ginger hair. The male was wearing a blue/purple t-shirt, blue jeans and black trainers. The male's face was completely putrefied and filled with maggots and so were both his hands. His arms were purple and his body cold. There is blood on the floor which appeared to come from his face where it had been eaten by maggots and flies."

Do I – do we – need to dwell in that room with the dead and decomposing Jack and his terrible smell and the maggots all over his face? I wasn't going to go share that with you because it's too terrible to share. But I've included it because this is the reality of suicide; the side we rarely see or read about. It's the bit in suicide memoirs and reports in the press that we draw a discreet veil over for obvious reasons. We talk about the terrible loss that comes in the wake of a suicide, but not its terrible look and its terrible smell.

As a society we need the stench of suicide in our nostrils; the horror of blood, the ravenous maggots and buzzing flies shoved in our collective face as an antidote to our culture's romanticism and moral acceptance of suicide. We focus so much on the tragedy of loss we have lost sight of the sheer horror of the act.

"There is a strange compulsive beauty to suicide, to the act, to the leap," writes Simon Critchley in his essay 'Notes on Suicide'. The artist Damien Hirst is quoted as having once said, "I think that suicide is the most perfect thing you can do in life."

The alleged 'beauty' that comes from suicides is due to its long association with suicidal poets, pop stars, tragic lovers and doomed writers. But we need to give suicide back its visceral repulsiveness. The *beauty* of suicide? The *perfection* of suicide? Come on guys. Have you seen a suicide close-up? Have you smelt the stench of a decaying loved one? I don't want to play the grieving dad card on Critchley and Hirst. Having a dead child gives you no special moral authority; your opinions shouldn't carry any more weight than anyone else's. But isn't there something not quite right about intellectuals and artists treating suicide as an *aesthetic* experience to appreciate and play around with?

Over the past one hundred years we have gone from moral condemnation of suicide to a non-judgemental accommodation, where the only stigma attached to suicide is *not* in our reluctance to talk about it – as everyone assumes – but to make moral judgments about it. It's taboo to say that suicide is *wrong* – morally, socially and culturally wrong – anymore.

But it's wrong and not because of some moralistic religiosity, but rather the pain it inflicts on loved ones is unimaginable and should be unacceptable. It is an act of self-murder that wounds everyone; the shrapnel from a suicide leaves family and friends scarred for life.

Is it possible that suicide has become too acceptable? It's not that our popular culture romanticises suicide so much as it *normalises* it. Suicide has lost its power to inspire fear and repugnance in people. It's not seen as a freakish or a bizarre thing to do. It's become almost like a lifestyle choice or a human right. The immediate go-to option of those who haven't even considered the alternatives or sought help.

The Kindness Of A Stranger

Living in Jack's house was a young woman called Emily who didn't know Jack well. Once in a while they'd pass each other by and exchange greetings. "He was always friendly," says Emily.

I can see Jack now, giving Emily a head flick of recognition and a soft, hiya as he passed her by in the hallway.

There was a moment that Sunday night when the other tenants and the police were outside the house, taking statements and waiting for the undertaker's car to arrive. It was then that Emily – who lived on the lower landing – found herself alone in the house with Jack's dead body upstairs. She could have left and gone off with her housemates. It must have been kind of spooky, being alone at night in that house with that strange dead guy upstairs.

But Emily didn't leave the house because she felt she should stay in her room and wait till someone came and took his body away. And when I asked her why, she told me: because it made her sad, thinking about Jack being upstairs in the house all alone; all dead and by himself.

"Maybe it's silly," said Emily, "but I was very upset for him and I didn't want to leave the house before they came to take him away."

In other words: she didn't want him to be lonely.

20

Fuck Therapy

I said I wouldn't do it. I said I was too smart for it. I said I could see through the spurious claims of therapy and grief counselling. I said I'd take my grief straight-up on the rocks and on the rack, without the sugar-coating comforts of therapeutic platitudes with their promises of closure and resolution, thank you very much.

I told myself I was saying yes to the old virtues of resilience and fortitude. I was accepting an ancient truth that we moderns seem to have lost: tragedies are intrinsic to human life. Or as we say these days: shit happens. And it's just a matter of time before shit happens to you.

And when it does there's no point in running off and seeking help and solutions from strangers and doctors. (We have friends and family for such hard times.) To do so is to fall for the great myth of modern life that for every problem there is a solution and for every pain a prescription for relief. Best to learn to endure the unendurable and fuck therapy!

Thinking this way gave my suffering a certain stoical valour. In effect I was saying: Look at me everyone, I stand alone silently, taking the slings and arrows of outrageous fortune in my stride! This was me playing the role of the tough guy; the strong and silent man; I sucked it up and held it in, while others spewed it out.

And now I find myself every Wednesday morning on the tube going to sit in a small room in Finchley with my therapist Nigel. I could have found a female therapist who was at least sexy or Jewish. Nigel is neither but he has a beard and a good brain.

I sit and talk and sometimes I cry. The way it works with therapy is this; you provide the tears and the therapist provides the box of tissues. But in my first session I noticed that Nigel had no box of tissues in his consulting room. Usually, the mandatory tissue box sits just out of sight of the patient, but within easy grasp. A sliver of tempting white untainted tissue spills out of the box's slit. They are meant to be a reassuring sight. These tissues are toilet paper for the heart; to wipe up after the emotional excrement has come out. But in this room there are no tissues. Is this an oversight or act of passive aggression on Nigel's part?

I put this to Nigel and he says, "a bit of both?"

Taking the tube to see my therapist reminds me of when in 2010 I used to take the tube with Jack to see his therapist – once a week – at the Priory in Roehampton. It was the last time I was really confident that things were going to work out for Jack. He was seeing a therapist he really liked, he was on medication that made him feel better, he was ready to return to his studies at University and we were getting along – and then it all fell apart.

On the train to my therapist I often talk to Jack. Actually, he talks to me.

Jack: Dad, you're wasting your time with therapy.

Me: Shut up Jack.

Jack: *I'm telling you, I know. I did loads of therapy – look what it did for me! Don't waste your time and money.*

Me: And what do you suggest I do instead?

Jack: *Get wasted! Get fucked! Get out of your head! Go out and have some fun! You're Mr. No Fun.*

Me: What do you mean? I have fun and I'm fun to be with!

Jack: *Man, don't take this the wrong way. I'm not having a go or anything, but you were never a fun sort of guy, were you?*

Me: What? I'm a fun guy! Aren't I?

Jack: *Naaa! You were always too serious.*

Me: Jesus! You sound just like my dad.

Jack: *Dad, why are you doing this therapy shit?*

Me: I just need to talk to someone.

Jack: *Dad, you can always talk to me. Wassup?*

Me: Gosh, I don't know. Let me think…umm…my son killed himself. My life is lonely. I'm fucking depressed. I keep breaking down and crying. So I thought it would be a good idea to talk to someone about things.

Jack: *Fair enough. But maybe I could help. On second thoughts, you never took any of my advice.*

Me: You never took any of mine! And don't forget you liked your first therapist at the Priory.

Jack: Yeah, he was a cool guy but he didn't exactly cure my problems, did he? Therapy never cured anyone. I met loads of people who had loads of therapy – and they were all fucking crazy!

Me: Yeah Jack that's true. But most of them are still alive.

● ● ●

Actually, I don't want to be in therapy in the first place; but I *need* to be in therapy. What do I hope to get out of it? I don't know. I'm stuck. I can't go back to my old life and I can't start a new one. I've gone into therapy not because I'm in pain, but because I'm feeling no pain. I'm numb. Confused. The coherence of my life story has collapsed. It makes no sense. I don't make sense. I don't see the point of anything. I don't see the point of not seeing the point either. I've given up.

I try to describe to Nigel what I'm feeling: I feel nothing. I have, I explain, entered a new phase I call, I Don't Give a Fuck (IDGAF). You don't have to be a Freud – or a Nigel – to see that I'm very depressed. But hey, don't knock depression. It does have its good points, at least my kind of I-Don't-Give-A-Fuck depression. It's like I've attained Zen enlightenment without the long sessions of back-aching meditation. I have found this liberating indifference to life. I'm no longer a prisoner of my desires. All the things I routinely worried about – money, work, love, loneliness – they don't matter because I don't give a fuck.

Nigel is not surprised by any of this. He explains that I have experienced a form of trauma. *Trauma?* That might seem obvious, but it wasn't to me. Trauma, I thought, is when you see some terrible life-changing thing happen, like when a child sees his father stab his mother to death or discovers his brother or sister hanging from a tree.

Nigel explained to me about my trauma; it was as if I'd taken a blow to the head. He said I had to give it time and that my mind was rebooting. Don't rush things, he advised. "You know how they're always saying don't just sit there, for heaven's sake do something? My advice is this – for heaven's sake just sit there and don't do anything."

That made a lot of sense to me. I had to give it time. I could see how I was trying to rush through this whole grieving experience. I wanted to put myself on trial, make a case for the defence and the prosecution, sum it all up, give my verdict of guilty or not guilty, take my punishment, do my time and move on. In short: I wanted to get it over with before it had even begun.

I tell Nigel about my difficulties with grieving and he tells me that's not surprising: "Your mind has erected very strong defences to protect you from pain."

So it doesn't necessarily mean that I didn't love my son?

That's right, says Nigel. But it's too early to say what is going on.

Nigel says I have to "recalibrate" my life. I have lost the old Cosmo. "Everything is up for grabs".

● ● ●

I must confess that I'd been in therapy before this time. During the Rocky period I insisted that Jack went to therapy. And whenever he came back from a session with his therapist, I'd ask him how it went and he'd say it was a waste of time or he couldn't remember what they talked about.

I got so fed up with this that I started going with Jack to his sessions to keep an eye on his progress and make a positive contribution. I remember one joint session where we discussed Jack's childhood and I learnt something that shocked me.

Jack didn't want to talk about his childhood, but his therapist insisted and got Jack to talk about his feelings as a child and his relations with his parents. I don't think Jack got much out of that session, but I did. I made an illuminating discovery: as a small boy he'd been scared of me because I was an angry, shouting dad.

Later, we walked back home in the late afternoon sunshine from the therapist's in silence. I wasn't angry by what Jack had said: I was shocked. Until that session at his therapist's I never realised just how unhappy he'd been as a child. I'd always thought that, on balance, I'd been a good and loving dad. As we arrived at our front door Jack said to me, "See, I told you therapy was a waste of time."

Once back home he asked me if it was ok if he got the sofa bed out and went to bed. Usually I wouldn't let him get into bed until evening time, but I said it was ok. So Jack went upstairs, pulled out the sofa bed and wrapped himself in his duvet and went online. I went to my room. I got into bed, wrapped myself in my duvet and went online. We both just lay in our separate rooms for the rest of the day and all of the night.

What a pair we were. Suicidal son and depressed dad, hiding under the covers; hiding from life and hiding from each other.

21

The Big Why?

Every suicide is a murder mystery waiting to be solved. But unlike the classic murder mystery of crime fiction or fact, with a suicide you find the corpse and the killer at the same time.

When you dig into the mystery of why, you rarely discover a conclusive answer that brings you the peace you crave. Instead you find a new trail of whys to wonder and worry about: why did he suffer so? Why did she think that suicide was the answer? Why was he so alone? Why didn't I do this? Why didn't I do that? Why?… Why?…Why?…

I have dozens of answers to a thousand-and-one whys? Here is a small selection I've contemplated over the years.

1   I was a bad dad who turned his back on his disturbed son.

2   He was a bad son who turned his back on his disturbed dad.

3   He was let down by doctors, the NHS and the marginalisation of mental health issues in our society.

4   He was a victim of men's inability to talk about their feelings.

5   He was killed by depression.

6   He was killed by loneliness.

7   He was killed by Jack.

JACK AND ME: HOW *NOT* TO LIVE AFTER LOSS

8   He was killed by me.

9   He was killed by you – you as a member of society.

10 He was killed by all of the above.

Of course, I wonder if the seeds of Jack's unhappiness – and eventual suicide – were planted in the break up of his parent's marriage and his unhappy childhood. The standard psychoanalytical/therapeutic view would be that with our break-up Jack experienced a traumatic sense of loss and abandonment. The theory goes – at least the version by the psychologist John Bowlby – that the child makes strong bonds of affection with the parents and these attachments provide safety and security. When they are broken the child often responds with intense anxiety, insecurity, hurt and anger. In other words, "your parents fuck you up, they don't mean to."

Psychoanalytical theory tells us one thing, but our experience of life tells us other stories and different truths. Plenty of children of divorced parents manage to build healthy, happy and fulfilled lives – just as children of happy marriages can end up like Jack.

Writing in *The Sunday Times* Jack's mother said: "I left his father when he was nine, but I don't blame myself: two of my best friends, exemplary and selfless mothers have raised sons with dreadful mental health problems, while I know far worse mothers than me who have raised robust, thriving sons."

I basically agree with that. But I think our break-up did have a negative impact on Jack. It made him anxious and fearful. Divorce always has some impact on kids – but that's not a reason why people should go on with unhappy marriages; for unhappy marriages can have a negative impact on kids too.

But just how negative the impact on Jack was I can't be sure. I often wonder if I think this way because it lets me off the hook. But I honestly don't believe that I'm to blame for my son's death; but neither can I be totally absolved of all responsibility.

The problem with the term blame is that it's too crude and simplistic a term to be of much use. What happens to an individual life – the way it turns out for good or bad – is too complex, too contradictory and too messy for the clear line of causality that allows the appropriation of blame.

That said, people desperately need an answer to the why question for it helps to make sense of what has happened. But maybe there is no answer – at least no singular, simple and certain answer to the Big Why? You can find all sorts of reasons for a suicide – financial, emotional, online bullying etc. – and yet it can remain an utter mystery. The suicide experts and charities and academics and parents of suicide – all these very dedicated, clever and compassionate people – assume that there is an answer to the Big Why?

But what if that's a false assumption?

We think we can find a cure for suicide like we can find a cure for cancer. But we don't have a cure for cancer and we probably never will; we have various effective treatments for cancer. Likewise, we don't have a cure for suicide; we have various effective ways of preventing suicide.

It's fair to say that we can identify "contributing factors" to suicide – sociological, economic, cultural and psychological – but establishing causal links between these factors and the individual act of suicide is much harder, if not impossible. We know why people commit suicide; but we don't know why certain individuals commit suicide..

The Samaritans have, over the years, conducted plenty of in-depth research into the causes of male suicide. While it has identified the factors that put men at risk – and men are more likely to die from suicide than women – it has found no clear causal explanation for suicide. Joe Ferns, executive director of policy for the Samaritans was refreshingly candid about the problem of causality. "It's difficult, but it's important we accept that we will probably never know the individual reasons behind individual cases."

• • •

I don't *blame* myself for Jack's death but I do have deep regrets. To get Jack through his troubles he needed more attentive care than I gave him in the final year of his life. I should have brought Jack home to live with me so I could keep an eye on him and give him a feeling of connection, of having a home – his home – where there was someone around who loved him.

Jack badly needed a calm and safe space; a shelter from the storms raging inside his head. I could have provided that, but I didn't want the headache of having Jack back living with me – and for that I'm ashamed. I remind myself that at the time I thought that Jack having his own place and being independent would be good for him.

Actually, I don't know if that would have made a great difference in the long run. It could have ended with me instead of his housemates in Harrow finding his body. But I do know that he was sick and in no position to live on his own way out in Harrow in that little white cube room of his.

I failed to see how deep and distressing his sense of isolation, loneliness, hurt and anger was. He once complained, "if someone had cancer you wouldn't treat them this way. I'm a sick person. I need help." He was right. I didn't treat him like a really sick person; I treated him like a boy with some very difficult problems that could be overcome if only he made an effort.

I was loving, patient and kind with Jack; but maybe not enough and not consistently. I can't say for certain that with more love and kindness I could have saved him. But there are very few certainties in life – and even fewer in death when it's by suicide.

If I had to point to one dominant factor to explain Jack's disturbed state of mind, I would say it was his use of drugs more than anything. The divorce might have been the kindling wood of future trouble – but drugs were what lit the flames.

• • •

Why do you young men like Jack kill themselves? The best explanation I've read for the act of suicide comes from the writer David Foster Wallace who killed himself in 2008. People like Jack are caught in what Wallace called an "invisible agony." This mental pain, writes Wallace, "reaches a certain unendurable level" causing the sufferer to kill themselves in, "the same way a trapped person will eventually jump from the window of a burning high-rise." Wallace makes an important point about such people; they are not fearless. "Make no mistake about people who leap from burning windows. Their terror of falling from a great height is still just as great as it would be for you or me standing speculatively at the same window just checking out the view. The variable here is the other terror, the fire's flames: when the flames get close enough, falling to death becomes the slightly less terrible of two terrors. It's not desiring the fall; it's terror of the flames."

Jack decided to kill himself because the flames in his mind were worse than his fear of the fall.

I think there is one key factor in explaining why some people pull back from the brink of death; why they step off the ledge or put down the rope and others don't: it's called hope. Those who have it, have a chance of living because hope offers an alternative to death.

But Jack had no hope. In 2015 he wrote in his *Rocky* statement that maybe he *could* get through his current difficulties, but he would have to live with the fear of "the next time my mind decided to short circuit and leave me adrift in a sea of emptiness and misery."

The things that can inoculate a person from the temptation of suicide – the bonds of love, a sense of purpose and meaning and being connected to people and the world at large – were all broken. We all have a suicide immune system within; Jack's had shut down. He had nothing inside to counteract the pro-death drive of loneliness, hurt, anger, depression and despair.

To actually kill yourself you must first kill the instinctual will to live. That isn't easy. You need something very powerful to push you over the line and break free from the gravitational pull of life and into the dark abyss of death. In the grip of his "invisible agony", Jack had no incentive or reason for turning back and taking that cable cord off his neck. On the contrary, he was convinced that nothing could help. Not medication. Not therapy. Not friends. Not family. Not love. Nothing was there waiting to help him. So why go back? Back is pain. Back is agony. Back is more of the same. His mind told him it all boils down to a simple equation: the past is pain. The present is pain. The future is pain. And death is the only solution to the pain of life.

It's amazing and terrifying the way a damaged mind can make such a convincing and rational case for its own extermination.

22

What Have I Done?

// Now comes the happy part of my story. The bit where I tell you about all the wonderful gifts my grief has given me and how it has enriched my life and helped me to grow spiritually and emotionally into a better and more fulfilled person. This is the happy part where I tell you about the work I've been doing to raise public awareness about mental health and suicide; about the cakes I've baked and the marathons I've run to raise money for suicide prevention charities. This is the happy bit about the charity I set up to honour Jack's memory. Did I not mention that? Have you not heard about my charity? It's called: *The Get Off Your Lazy Arse and Do Something Good Foundation*. It raises money and awareness about useless dads like me who do nothing but devote themselves to the pleasures of self-pity and self-flagellation. In other words, after three years I've not changed."

That was my conclusion to this book, which I finished in 2018. I was a Do Nothing Dad who felt a mix of self-contempt (for not doing anything) and a sense of superiority for…well, not doing anything. When I read personal stories about growth through grief I wasn't inspired to change; I was inspired to sneer.

For example, *The Guardian's* one-time grief columnist, who went by the pseudonym of Adam Golightly, wrote that since the death of his wife, "I am probably kinder, calmer, a better father, more fulfilled professionally, will live longer and am better equipped to support my fellow bereaved."

And I thought: *yeah right, I bet you are*! But the satisfactions of sneering at others are shallow and self-defeating. Sooner or later you'll have to stop clinging to the comfort blanket of cynicism and face the question: what now? How do I live after loss?

Golightly's change was a challenge to me and is a challenge to everyone who has or will experience loss. For a long time, I tried to dismiss his claims but one thought kept coming back to me: if he could change, why not me? I had no clever comeback to that.

I also resented the idea that people in my situation were blessed with some sort of special insight or wisdom about life as a result of their loss. "If you know about loss you know about family and about love, survival and resilience and strength. *If you know about loss you know about life* (my italics)", wrote the journalist Julia Moorehouse.

Oh really? What exactly does loss teach you about love, survival and resilience? I'd experienced loss but I knew nothing about these things – well, not anything new or profound that I didn't know before. I knew back then about the fragility and preciousness of human life and all the other life-affirming truths that death leaves in its wake.

But instead of really thinking about this deeply and bringing it into my life, I dismissed it with another wise crack: "Reader, is there anything more annoying and useless than retrospective wisdom? I hate the way it turns up too late, like a guest at a party that was over hours ago – and yet expects a big round of applause for put-ting in an appearance."

It was only when I learned to shut up, stop trying to be clever and let Jack's death speak to me that I realised that loss does have something to teach us about life. Put simply: all that existential doubt and anxiety about the meaning/purpose of life can disappear in the wake of loss. You *know* what it's all about.

The distracting fog of daily life lifts and you see with great clarity and certainty what really matters in life – love, people – and how to live your life (with love and kindness). And that's it. That's the only gift that grief gives you – but that's good enough.

The trouble is that death wakes us up to life; but life lulls us back to sleep; if we let it. The passage of time – which helps us to heal – also helps us to forget the wisdom we found. Before you know it you're back in the forgetful fog of daily life. The To Do list replaces the To Be List. It takes a great effort to conquer the amnesia of loss. We need rites and rituals to help us remember and that's why I'm starting to celebrate Jack's birthday and mourn his death.

But have I changed?

I think so and for the better. About two years after Jack's death someone asked me what I'd learned from the experience? It was a question that made me uncomfortable. Learn what? Why do people assume there's always a lesson to be learned? What could I say: suicide is a bummer? Don't try this at home, kids? So I just said, "not much".

About a year ago someone asked the same sort of question and instead of going for the easy option of "duh, I don't know!" and changing the conversation, I thought about it and said: "this is what I've learned from Jack's death and I hope it will be of some help to you: *you can lose anyone at any time…just like that!*" And here for dramatic effect, I snapped my fingers. I try to think about that truth every day and every time I see a friend.

And I have talked to friends with troubled children like Jack and made suggestions and offered comfort where I can. The mother of one young man, who so reminds me of Jack, told me she thought I had helped her son and had certainly helped her. At one time I would have said nothing because I assumed I had nothing to say. So yes, I've made a little progress.

• • •

Why was I so resistant to change – so hostile to the idea that my grief could lead me to something good? At the time I wrote, "My pain is the umbilical cord that ties me to Jack. I don't want closure or to get over his death; I want to keep him close to me. I'm like one of those parents who, having lost a child, keep their child's bedroom exactly the way it was before they died: only I'm the unchanged room."

But this wasn't true because I had not kept Jack close to me after his death. And now I think I have the answer: I could not create a new and better future for myself because I hadn't come to terms with the past. I couldn't face Jack or face myself – so I just shut the whole thing down. I decided it was the end of the story of Jack and me; but in fact a new chapter was just beginning. Only, I didn't want to write it and I didn't want to live it.

But now I'm ready to keep changing. I'm ready to grow – the fact that I can use that word grow and not gag, shows that I'm growing! And I think that on balance I have changed for the better. But can I, like Adam Golightly, claim to be a better dad, calmer, and more able to help others in my situation?

Without being complacent – or conceited – I think I can. Since Jack's death I have worked on my anger, taken up meditation, practiced breathing, studied Buddhist teachings on non-reactivity, spent time doing charity work – and yes, I'm still an angry dumb dickhead and very inadequate dad! But compared to what I was? There are signs of small incremental improvements with the passing of time. The bottom line is this: I'm *trying* to do better.

• • •

One thing I have discovered is that we deal with the reality of loss only *after* it happens, when we should be dealing with that reality before it happens. After all, you and everyone you know will, eventually, die. We are all facing the same death sentence and the only difference is timing and the manner of our execution. So doesn't it make more sense to see the preciousness and fragility of human life *before* someone you love dies? The loving eulogy we will give at their funeral is nice, but it's a bit late isn't it?

The loving eulogy should be for the living and not the dead.

Lately, I've been telling very close friends that I love them, and yes I'm always sober. I've discovered that you can't tell an English person you love them without them wanting to die of embarrassment. Some of them just pretend not to have heard me. Some say, "Ahhh. That's sweet," and quickly change the topic. Men usually laugh, nervously. I don't want to get all huggy and gooey with people; I just don't want to ever have to worry that I didn't tell someone I loved that I loved them – before it was too late. There are few regrets in life as big and long-lasting as that one.

This is important not only for our loved ones but ourselves. How we treat them before they die will influence how we treat ourselves after they die. We need to be as loving, kind and patient as we can possibly be, so in the wake of loss we can be loving, patient and as kind to ourselves. If that strikes you as too "touchy-feely", just wait till you lose a loved one and you're choking on your guilt and regrets for not having been more "touchy-feely".

● ● ●

I was so focused on the possibility of Jack ending his life that I never spent any time thinking about my life after his death. What would a life without Jack be like? (Yes, there were times of total exasperation when I would have said "great!") But I would never have said that, had I really thought deeply about what a life where Jack would exist only as an urn full of ashes, stashed away in my cupboard.

If only I could have stepped back and calmed my anger and realised that the maddening boy before me will die – by his own hand or by life – and then ask myself: *how do we treat the dying*? If I could have done that things would have been different. I'm not saying Jack would still be alive, but our relationship after his death would have been better.

Chill, Dad

I think the most valuable thing I've learnt from writing this book is a piece of very wise advice that came from an unlikely source: Jack.

Jack: Really? What was that – get wrecked? Get pissed? Kill yourself?

No Jack. You told me that whenever I got angry or anxious, I should just chill!

Jack: Wise words indeed! Too bad you never took my advice. But then you were the most un-chilled dad in the universe. Do you even know what it means?

• • •

To chill is to relax. To stay cool. Be calm. It is grace under pressure. It's a voice that never shouts, an ear that listens deeply and a mind that responds with thoughtful care – but I dismissed it as one of those dumb dopey things that teenagers say like, whatever.

But I realise that all through my life loved ones have been saying the same thing to me in various ways. My dad used to say, "Lighten up!" My mother tried to get me to "Zen-off", by which she meant not to get entangled in the melodramas of the mind and try to take a more detached and Zen view. My brother would say, "Relax man, you're too uptight. Don't be so melodramatic!"

The command to "chill" sounds too simplistic to be of any use, but the complexity of the concept comes in the difficult practice of staying cool. It's a concept we can all understand; but it's a practice few of us can do successfully.

It's impossible for me to measure the amount of unnecessary anger, hurt and psychological damage I have generated over the years not only with Jack but other loved ones – simply by my failure to chill. I can honestly say that had I chilled I would have been a better man, a better husband and a better dad.

• • •

I take comfort in imagining that Jack would have forgiven me for my numerous failings. I used to worry that I'd never said sorry to Jack, and then it was too late. But in researching this book I found this email, which was sent on 8 April 2015 – over two months before his death – and was the last email I ever sent him. Here's what I wrote:

Dear Jack,

I'm so sorry that we had a row again. I know this is hard for you to believe but I only want to help you and I always seem to end up hurting you. Sorry I yelled. I wish I could control my anger and my exasperation and never shout at you. And sometimes I manage to do that – but not often enough. It must be very distressing for you. I know that you need love and patience and care from your family. I want to provide that. But I do feel that you also need to be jolted out of a negative mindset that stops you from making a nice life for yourself. You're right, your mind is damaged – and that's because you believe that your mind is damaged and that nothing can be done to repair it. You say you've tried everything. I disagree. But I know I can't convince you so I'll let it go. Anyway, whenever you are ready to make up, I am too.

Cosmo

And here's what Jack wrote back:

Yeah, it's cool. Don't worry about it.

I like to think that was Jack forgiving me, and that we had made our peace. But maybe it was his way of saying fuck you I don't want to talk about it. That's what suicide leaves you with; a thousand maybes and a million I-don't-knows.

And yet I have found a kind of peace with Jack. I still think he did a terrible thing and it was the wrong decision. But I'm no longer angry at him for doing it and for not writing a suicide note or saying goodbye to me.

I'm not going to go all soft and tell you that I've discovered what a beautiful, brilliant and golden-boy Jack was, and how he enriched all of our lives. Jack was, at times, an arsehole. A complete idiot. A thief. A liar. A lazy shit…or at least the Other Jack was and I can't now pretend he didn't exist. But then we all have a bit of The Other Jack inside of us? The Other Me – Cosmo – is not exactly a pretty sight either.

But that Other Jack no longer dominates the way I think about him. I see a scared, sad and anxious boy who had so much kindness and love in him but the forces of anger, anxiety and hurt took over and his better self got lost. My mistake then was not to see him as a complex person of many parts: I only saw Jack and his problems. But people are not their problems. When we stick a label or diagnosis on someone that's how we see them. The part – the troubling part that causes parents distress – becomes greater than the whole.

Without Jack in my life things are easier. There's less worry, stress, less conflict, less anger and frustration. Life is more comfortable but also more empty. His suicide means we have lost the life we shared and we have lost the life we would have shared as he got older.

But I miss my Jack. I say that knowing that if he were to walk through the door right now we'd hug and I would say how sorry I was – and we'd probably be having our first row within fifteen minutes. But so what? We could hang out and watch movies and listen to music. Hey, maybe we could get high together and have a few laughs? I'd even watch *The Texas Chainsaw Massacre* with him.

I used to worry that I no longer loved my son, but I don't think I ever stopped loving him. I think it's possible to lose sight of your love for someone – but that doesn't mean that the love is gone forever. Other things – problems, rows, anger – just get in the way and we lose sight of them and our love.

As for my problem with grieving, it was another example of me trying to live up to an idea – in this case, what a grieving dad should be like. I think I have been grieving for Jack ever since he died – and will do so for the rest of my life; but I do it slowly and quietly. Grief doesn't have to express itself in a big cathartic outburst of pain. It doesn't have to be an explosion or a terrifying scream; it can be as soft and quiet as a prayer.

And finally, the question I now have to face is this: have I written the book I promised I would never write? That is, the safe, soft sentimental memoir of loss that ties a big bow around the tragic story of a boy's suicide?

I hope not – but that's for you the reader to decide. Maybe in reaction to my initial cynicism I went too far the other way into an uncritical optimism. I want to offer some hope; but hope based on hard truths about love, death and being a parent. There is the danger that the grief of others becomes appropriated for our own lack of feeling; we get off on the intensity of raw emotion. Feeling bad makes us feel good because it makes us feel more alive. That was what my cynicism kept me safe from. And now I'm happy to let go of the old cynical me. I'm happy to say that there is life after loss and it can be better than the one we lived before.

23

The Urn Returns

I did it. Just now. I just went and got the urn from the cupboard; and here it is by my side. (It's not brown as I said before, but more plum coloured. And it's not as heavy as I remember.) And I don't feel all spooky or spiritual. And I don't feel sad. I just feel relieved.

I open the lid and see that Jack's ashes are wrapped in a plastic bag. I open the bag and spoon out two heaps of grey ash onto a small white dish. It looks like kitty litter. Do I dare touch it? I take a pinch between my thumb and forefinger; instead of feeling a fine powdery substance it's more grainy than ashy. (That must be from the wood of his coffin.)

Today – the 20th of May 2022 – is Jack's birthday. He would have been thirty-eight years old. I can't say that had he lived anything would have been better for him or between us. But it couldn't have got worse and at least he would be alive, and just to be alive would be enough for me.

I put the lid back on the urn, but left out the little dish of Jack ash. And then, I hold the urn in my arms, press it close to me like I did when Jack was a baby. I say a little prayer and tell Jack how much I love him and miss him – and from now on I will do this on his birthday.

The urn is going back into its original corner in my sitting room and the little plate of Jack ash is staying on the mantelpiece.

So when visitors ask, "what's that in the dish? I will say: "Oh, have you not met my son Jack?"

Jack: Good one dad! That will freak 'em out!

Me: We can but try. So, you always wanted to come home – and now here you are. Happy?

Jack: Yeah. But knowing you, you'll probably lose it, shout at my ashes and chuck out the urn – only kidding!

Me: No, I won't. Though one day I will have to spread them somewhere. Any preferences?

Jack: Yeah, Camden Town. Find the sleaziest drug-saturated dump full of fucked-up crazies and lay me to rest there! (Laughs)

Me: You know something? I've missed you.

Jack: Ahhh! That's nice. Are we going to have a father-son moment?

Me: I just want to say…I wish I'd been a better dad to you.

Jack: Please, don't beat yourself up. You were a good dad.

Me: Really?

Jack: Naah. I just said that to make you feel better.

Me: Oh.

Jack: Dad, I'm just fucking with you. It's all good.

Me: Seriously, I lost sight of what was great about you. I think I've found it again. I promise I won't let it or you go.

Jack: Cheers.

Me: Now what happens?

Jack: Dad, can I ask you one favour?

Me: No! You can't borrow £20!

Jack: Chill man! Just asking!

Ends

Author's Thanks

I want to thank Piers Blofeld and Eugenie Furniss for all their brave attempts to find a publisher for this book.

Also, a big thanks to Clare Conville for all her encouragement and advice.

Thanks to Helen Hawkins and Jenny McCartney for helping me to keep the faith in moments of doubt.

Thanks to Alice Squires for her love and wisdom during a tough time.

Thanks to Ellie Hind and Jane Collins for diligent proofreading.

But my biggest thanks goes to Todd Swift for having the courage to say "Yes!" when everybody else in publishing had said "No!"

Cosmo Landesman
August 2022